# ARCHITECTURE IN ISLAMIC SOCIETIES

Edited by Cynthia C. Davidson

with 253 illustrations 119 in colour

The Aga Khan Award for Architecture

**THAMES AND HUDSON**

# Acknowledgments

The process that made this book possible began more than twenty years ago when His Highness The Aga Khan announced the creation of the Aga Khan Award for Architecture. His vision was to focus on projects for Islamic societies around the world. It was an extraordinary and unprecedented gesture that has raised the level of discussion about architecture around the globe. This book marks the seventh time that the Award has been given, and an international network of individuals has contributed to it, from the members of the Steering Committee and the Master Jury to the team of Technical Reviewers. The hands-on work was accomplished by dedicated members of the staffs of the Aga Khan Award for Architecture and the Aga Khan Trust for Culture, who laboured under extremely tight time constraints. At the Trust, Helen Goodman and William O'Reilly; at the Award, Jack Kennedy, Farrokh Derakhshani, Shiraz Allibhai, Marco Christov, Françoise Rybin and Christine Garnier. I am grateful, too, to Suha Özkan, secretary general of the Award, for the trust he placed in me to edit this book, and for the opportunity he has given me to participate in this exciting programme. Finally, I want to thank Thames & Hudson, especially Lucas Dietrich, Catherine Hall and designer Aaron Hayden, whose support led us to this final volume. – CCD

HALF-TITLE PAGE Rehabilitation of Hebron Old Town
TITLE PAGE Tuwaiq Palace, Riyadh, Saudi Arabia

# Contents

The Aga Khan Award for Architecture **6**

Introduction: *The Pragmatics of Resistance* Cynthia C. Davidson **7**
*The Conscience of Architecture* Romi Khosla **12**
*Continuity in a Changing Tradition* Saleh Al-Hathloul **18**
*Pragmatism and the Built Environment* Arif Hasan **32**

The Recipients of the 1998 Award **36**

Rehabilitation of Hebron Old Town **38**

Slum Networking of Indore City, Indore, India **54**

Lepers Hospital, Chopda Taluka, India **66**

Salinger Residence, Selangor, Malaysia **82**

Tuwaiq Palace, Riyadh, Saudi Arabia **96**

Alhamra Arts Council, Lahore, Pakistan **114**

Vidhan Bhavan, Bhopal, India **128**

Master Jury Discussion **144**
*The Aga Khan Award as a Process of Thinking* Mohammed Arkoun **152**
*Legacies of the Future* Suha Özkan **158**
Project Data and Personnel **168**

The 1998 Steering Committee **171**
The 1998 Master Jury **172**
The 1998 Award Technical Review **174**

# The Aga Khan Award
# for Architecture

FRONT ROW (**from left**):
Charles Jencks, Selma Al-Radi, Saleh Al-Hathloul, Prince Hussain Aga Khan, Her Highness The Begum Aga Khan, His Highness The Aga Khan, Dogan Tekeli, Mohammed Arkoun, Zaha Hadid, Adhi Moersid

SECOND ROW (**from left**):
Arif Hasan, Yuswadi Saliya, Peter Eisenman, Balkrishna V. Doshi, Ali Shuaibi, Romi Khosla, Azim Nanji, Arata Isozaki, Suha Özkan, Fredric Jameson

The Aga Khan Award for Architecture is one part of the Aga Khan Trust for Culture, a private, non-denominational, philanthropic foundation which conducts three major programmes: the Aga Khan Award for Architecture, the Historic Cities Support Programme, and the Education and Culture Programme.

The Aga Khan Trust for Culture is an integral part of the Aga Khan Development Network, a family of institutions created by His Highness The Aga Khan, with distinct yet complementary mandates to improve the welfare and prospects of people in countries in the developing world, particularly in Asia and Africa.

The Award is organized on a three-year cycle, and is governed by a Steering Committee chaired by His Highness The Aga Khan. Awards totalling up to US $500,000 – the largest architectural prize in the world – are made every three years to projects selected by an independent Master Jury. The Award has completed seven cycles of activity since 1977, and over seventy building projects have been recognized, including the seven recipients of the 1998 Award which are featured in this volume.

# Introduction
## The Pragmatics of Resistance

Cynthia C. Davidson

In the context of cultural production today, architecture is commonly thought to be a response to what needs to be done or should be done, not what *could be*, whether it is done or not. Things that make architecture happen, such as tools, money, policy, originate in the so-called realm of the pragmatic, the real-life conditions that bear on the making of architecture. Architecture, in fact, is the pragmatic art: it must resist gravity, it must provide shelter, it must accommodate a social function. But as a social function, architecture is never truly free of ideological or political associations, whether or not those associations are symbolized or accommodated by or in a specific project. Thus 'what could be' becomes the possibility for a moral and critical standard that allows one to hold society's needs and architecture's response to them up to scrutiny. It offers a speculative, theoretical opening for a discipline that otherwise flourishes in precise and definite terminology.

Since the first primitive hut, architecture as a social practice has provided shelter for social groups, which in turn formed communities. Romi Khosla suggests in this volume that architecture today has become imbued with a new social conscience, which is also an increasingly important theme in the Aga Khan Award for Architecture. This idea of a social conscience leads to what could be described as an emerging or new pragmatism, one which also embodies a moral and critical dimension. It is not the same social agenda or conscience that imbued the ideology of early modernism, however.

The difference is important. In the early twentieth century, European modernism evolved as an ideological social project, seeking to remake social institutions. Khosla elaborates the gradual erosion of modernism's social and ideological agenda after World War II and attributes the cause to the socialist project's internal contradictions. But it was also the success of modernism's formal project that led to its consumption by global capital and allowed for the mass production of generic repetitive units at a lower cost and at a rapid rate.

The tabula rasa condition that was integral to modernist thought, a clearing away in order to enact its ideological project, is neither possible nor necessary in developing societies. The hierarchical social orders embedded in Western societies for two centuries are not entrenched in the same way in Islamic societies. There, architects must make do with given conditions, must weave their work into an existing urban fabric. Projects are by nature additive, their gestures more responsive to, rather than standing apart from, their contexts.

In his essay here, Arif Hasan describes this condition as a certain pragmatism that is necessary in order to implement building programmes in most indigent communities, as well as in politically compromised urban situations. Hasan proposes a four-point agenda for action, which assumes that problems require solutions. His agenda, while clearly necessary, may not offer a moral or critical resistance to a given condition, or any opportunity for exploring 'what could be'. However, it can be seen as part of a new, emerging pragmatism that has another, more important function: it stands as a form of resistance to the insatiable spread of global capital.

The evolution of global capital and the ensuing development of a global economy with Western origins has also introduced a new kind of pragmatism, one based on investment and profitable returns. This pragmatism has led to a new kind of architecture, one that finds its energies in infrastructure, operational systems, and organizations of mass. These kinds of projects seem to lose not only their specificity of place but also their social meaning. For example, the explosion of mass housing developments appears to be based on the goal of investment for profit rather than in creating socially cohesive communities. This architecture is indistinguishable from its generic prototypes and typologies, and its meaning is further reduced by the kitsch appliqué of regional pastiche.

According to the American urbanist Saskia Sassen, a specific geography has emerged to accommodate globalization. 'The space constituted by the global grid of cities,' she writes, 'a space with new economic and political potential, is perhaps one of the most strategic spaces for the formation of transnational identities and communities. . . The transmigration not only of capital but also of people . . . takes place in this global grid. It is a space for the transmigration of cultural forms, for the reterritorialization of "local" subcultures.'[1] This causes one to ask, does this transmigration of cultural forms carry with it a moral and critical argument? Further, do transmigration and reterritorialization and the speed at which the global economy is pushing both of these developments begin to uproot and eradicate patterns of social organization in a systematic way? To offer resistance to this global phenomenon is not to run from its path because it has no clear path, no trajectory. It can only be countered perhaps from within, with a form of socially conscious architecture that suggests 'what could be'.

This pragmatism from within is neither a 'third way' of thinking about architecture nor an oppositional strategy. Rather, it is an attempt to come to terms with the privatization of the state and the central debates of our time – not withdrawing from them. By accepting and thus working from within the conditions of global capital it may be possible to produce a moral and critical resistance – which today cannot be distanced from modes of production – to find a future that can no longer be cloaked in idealism; rather, it is a future grounded in a new pragmatic of material reality. The equation of utopian idealism with moral responsibility contributed to the downfall of the social project of modernism. Today, within the prospect of material reality, it is also possible to have a critical project.

Architecture, so bounded by pragmatism, cannot effect change either within its own discipline or in society at large without a moral judgment, a social conscience. As a whole, the work in this book begins to suggest 'what could be' in socially conscious forms of resistance to the pragmatics of globalization. This does not mean that all forms of specific, regional material characteristics are resistant to globalization. Nor does it mean that all forms of abstract modernism are consumed by mass production. The distinction being made here is neither for or against the regional vernacular or the abstract modern. Rather, it is an idea of resistance that contains a singularity, that is, a difference from the dominant forces of any era. The moral and social conscience suggested in this volume is one form of such a resistance today.

[1]Saskia Sassen, 'Reconfiguring Centrality' in *Anywise*, ed. Cynthia C. Davidson (Cambridge, Massachusetts: The MIT Press, 1996), 131.

# Report of the 1998 Award Master Jury

The nine members of the Master Jury for the Aga Khan Award for Architecture met three times to select the winners from the 424 projects that were presented in the Award's seventh cycle. After the second meeting, twenty-four of these projects were reviewed on site by a team of twelve distinguished reviewers, whose presentations made the Jury aware of the many complex aspects of each project.

From the beginning of its deliberations, the Jury was concerned with recognizing projects that had a wider global context and meaning, as well as with identifying those projects that had regional relevance. It was also concerned not to duplicate messages conveyed through selections by earlier juries, thus the absence of certain types of work in this Award cycle needs to be understood in that spirit.

The Jury searched for projects which respond creatively to the new crisis situations in the world in general today and in the Muslim world in particular: demographic pressure, environmental degradation, globalization, standardization, ethnic tensions, the crisis of the nation-state, the struggle for democracy and human rights, and the like. This search was related to community rebuilding, on the one hand, and to the development of vital modern vernacular styles on the other. The Jury recognized that major social, economic and political changes are taking place in the world today and that the countries of the Islamic world are being profoundly affected by these changes. They are developing new lifestyles, cultural values, symbols and aspirations. The relationships between classes and groups are changing, as well as those between governments and the people at large. Except for social projects, an architecture that reflects these new realities has yet to be recognized. The Award, as a result of its history, is in an ideal position to initiate this discourse.

Seven projects were selected for the Award. Two were seen to have qualities that could be of relevance to a broader, global context; the Rehabilitation of Hebron Old Town and the Slum Networking of Indore City were considered exceptional in ways that are a departure from the conventional approach to upgrading. Both share the idea of reclaiming community space from growing social, physical and environmental degradation. In the case of Hebron, the project was initiated and managed by a community under siege.

Two projects were seen to respond in an exceptional way to specific social and environmental conditions. The Salinger Residence, an example of excellent architecture, uses local materials and skills to create a spatial vocabulary which is contemporary and yet not alienated from its specific cultural context. The Lepers Hospital, on the other hand, is sensitively designed to respond to the needs of the outcasts of society, providing them with shelter and hope while using minimum resources. Its architectural form is unpretentious and its proportions and concepts are of the highest order.

Three projects, the Tuwaiq Palace, the Alhamra Arts Council and the Vidhan Bhavan, are important large-scale public buildings. Their form and context were regarded by the Jury as very significant in the continuous process of evolving a contemporary architectural vocabulary within the Islamic world. Their public functions and the relatively large scale of their volumes inevitably add to their importance as social catalysts within their respective societies.

Geneva, 12 June 1998

## Recipients of the 1998
## Aga Khan Award for Architecture

Rehabilitation of Hebron Old Town

Slum Networking of Indore City, India

Lepers Hospital, Chopda Taluka, India

Salinger Residence, Selangor, Malaysia

Tuwaiq Palace, Riyadh, Saudi Arabia

Alhamra Arts Council, Lahore, Pakistan

Vidhan Bhavan, Bhopal, India

# The Conscience of Architecture

There is a prevalent view that the Aga Khan Award for Architecture is concerned with promoting a third debate in architecture. This debate, articulated, for instance, so clearly by Charles Jencks in 1995, argues that the Award is 'the third way – the veritable multi-laned highway' that is pluralistic and hence identifies architectural projects that span a wide range of typologies. By giving approbation to the modern Institut du Monde Arabe in Paris as well as the mud Great Mosque at Niono, the Award is seen to encompass 'multi-laned' contemporary architectural activities that could be relevant to the developing Islamic world. Since the Award recognizes conservation projects, social housing and innovative contemporary architecture as well as other types of work, it does seem to have become the symbol of a broad, pluralistic architectural patronage. The Award's third position is defined in the context of the transatlantic debate about modernism, at one end, and the regional debates on authenticity, cultural continuity and craftsmanship, at the other. This so-called third position is supposed to occupy the middle ground between these two debates and also to promote debate and an exchange of ideas that try to reconcile the two seemingly irreconcilable positions. Dubbing the Award 'middle ground', 'third way' and 'pluralistic' is therefore easy to understand. Over the last seven cycles, the Award has recognized more than seventy projects in different parts of the world. With every Jury Report that explains the reasons for choosing the projects, the message of the Award is broadened and diversified. The societies that form the constituency of the Award are themselves very diverse, thus the Award takes care to publish its juries' deliberations and reasons in the form of debates on issues that can bring together diverse concerns for diverse societies.

The third way is one way of seeing the Award as part of the newly emerging, seemingly pluralistic direction in architecture that includes modernism, regionalism, housing, conservation of historical buildings, urban planning and landscaping. This image of the Award is a 'comfortable' or easily acceptable one that would please and make sense to the largest number of people. Since it is culturally and stylistically non-specific and represents more a basket of ideas than the sharp edge of a specific viewpoint about architecture in a global context, the Award's position in the global debate can be interpreted as one that shifts.

The global debate is an important reference point because it presumes not only global participants but also participants who are engaged in a debate about core issues relevant to architects. The global debate is generated by the engines of private capital, which are geographically located in the West. They provide the essential ingredients of the debate, which are patronage, media coverage and engagements in a critical discourse. The media constitute a global network; thus architectural events such as the inauguration of the Guggenheim Museum at Bilbao, Spain, become global events.

Lepers Hospital

# Romi Khosla

Tuwaiq Palace

This dynamic partnership between the media and architecture is a recent phenomenon. Media as a whole has its own requirements, and for architecture to be important it must be iconic, a clearly identified product, the centrepiece of debate and, of course, politically significant.

The nature of the global debate about architecture has changed significantly in the last two decades. During the fifty years after the Russian Revolution, the central debate that concerned post-Bauhaus architecture was primarily about the ideology of modernism and its international significance. Until the early 1970s, even though postwar capitalism had restructured itself and Europe had significantly recovered from the damage of World War II, the ideological content of modernism was concerned with avant-garde positions and proposals based on the socialist ideas of reformulating societies. Municipal housing proposals, leisure activities and urban-scale projects were concerned with reformulating futures, which had always been an important concern of socialism. However, the socialist project could not recover from its internal contradiction. As the process of collapse began with the Soviet tanks entering Budapest, it gained momentum until *perestroika* and *glasnost* finally dismantled it completely. As the process of discrediting the socialist project gained strength, it became increasingly difficult to defend egalitarian futures as architectural ideas. While capitalism restructured itself and put an end to its internal rivalries – which had precipitated the war – and as the epoch of Pax Americana began to gain momentum, the social concerns of architects were dispersed in diverse directions. The New Left emerged as the symbol of resistance to the increasingly privatized West and tried to bundle together the dispersed pluralistic issues about regional identities, the environment and resistance movements that had broken away from the communist ideology in the 1960s. Successive conservative governments then began to tear down the social security nets and infrastructure and let them out to the private sector. The state was replaced by the private sector as the more significant patron, and the architectural profession lost its most important client. In the decades following the implementation of privatization all over Europe, the corporate clients emerged as the champions of modern architecture and architects had little option but to narrow their concerns and jettison the inconvenient ideological stance that promoted ideal egalitarian futures. In a sense, the architectural debate became detached from the central debates about culture, social and economic issues and futures in Western societies. Having lost contact with the New Left, modern architecture began to be deeply enmeshed in corporate architecture and the crafting of new building materials.

The new corporate clients of architecture stripped modern architecture of its social concerns but hailed and encouraged its great formal qualities and its potential

Salinger Residence

'signature status'. International finance capital, faced with underlying unemployment and accompanied by sluggish growth rates in almost all advanced countries, turned to the untapped market of the millions of potential Asian consumers. International financial institutions rode out for opportunities in Asia and launched massive architectural projects in Southeast Asia and southern China, which are nearing completion. Modern architecture, now on a back burner in the social debate, became an inseparable partner in the economic development of Bangkok, Shanghai, Canton and a host of other coastal centres in Asia where capital arrived from the West in search of higher returns. The buildings that responded to the growing needs of the finance sector became major icons in the banking world. They exhibited a wide range of stylistic hues, but they also belonged securely to modernity.

These are the mega-projects of today. At one time, Tony Garnier and Le Corbusier had visualized the mega-projects of modernism as the ideal cities of the industrial workers. The Asiatic and particularly the coastal urban developments of Canton and Shanghai see these contemporary mega-projects as the new territorial conquests of international finance. They are international in their funding, design, construction and staffing, but their achievements do not seem to form any part of the global critique of architecture. Nowhere are the architectural programmes of these mega-projects linked to concerns about the people whom socialism championed.

It remains apparent that enormous poverty is still prevalent in the Asiatic world as well as in the Islamic world. Concerns about their condition and future cannot simply disappear or become charitable questions just because the socialist project has disappeared. Perhaps the Award represents the only, and rather lonely, articulated position that holds that architects still have broader responsibilities in developing societies. It is just possible that the Award is *not* trying to carve a 'third way' that spans from modernism to tradition. Instead, it is possible that the Award's importance lies in clearly articulating an alternative debate about the relevance of architecture today. It seems apparent that the Award is questioning the narrowing of the debate in 'modern' architecture and is instead considering talking about a contemporary architecture that is more relevant to the problems of development. This would naturally influence the choice of geographical areas where such a debate could be relevant. By confining its search to the boundaries of the Islamic world, the Award is virtually signalling its own

Alhamra Arts Council

constituency as being at least one contemporary world where the broader social issues of architecture can be practised and discussed.

These broad concerns are going to become crucial to the global condition in the next millennium. It is possible to argue that the social concerns that award-winning projects reflect are globally relevant. African economies have collapsed because the social food security system was devastated. The entire former socialist block is experiencing downward-spiralling economies that have reached a precarious situation, with unemployment as high as 30 per cent in places where 'structural adjustments' are being hammered into place. Millions of precast multistorey housing blocks, jerry-built in the 1960s and 1970s, are beginning to crack and flake. This enormous region, on the border of Europe, has had its national income reduced to a third of its former size; its enormous social infrastructure, built over the years, has all but collapsed; poverty is rampant; and mafia gangs control the economy. In the coming millennium, these are the places where societies have to be given new futures. These new futures cannot and will not emerge out of the patronage of international finance capital. It is possible, however, that these futures can be articulated by the broader concerns about architecture that give importance to community involvement: craft, rebuilding of old urban centres, social housing and self-help. The Award could be considered as a keeper of the conscience of architecture, documenting in its debates and published materials the relevance of architecture in developing societies.

In its announcements of winners over the last seven cycles, the Award has identified a wide range of projects, with each jury shifting its emphasis in different directions. However, common to all these directions is the concern about the past, present and future. By including conservation, social projects and innovative contemporary buildings within its terms of reference, the Award has defined a broader perspective of architecture that could be important to formulate now that the transatlantic architectural debates have become strongly influenced by the interests of global finance and media projection. The Award uses an elaborate system of identifying projects for its consideration. Nominations followed by Technical Reviews and a series of jury meetings for each cycle ensure that a project is not simply viewed as an abstract model of form. The context, function, social relevance and regional importance are all considered criteria for excellence. By a process of inclusion rather than exclusion, the Award has been able to identify a reforestation project in Turkey as well as a lepers' hospital in India that used the minimum resources to create a structure for the benefit of the outcasts of society.

Despite the clear intentions of the Award to formulate its own message in the world of architecture, the impact of its significance in the global debate remains somewhat difficult to identify. Although successive juries have been concerned with trying to

Vidhan Bhavan

Slum Networking of Indore City

measure the contribution of the Award's message to the international architectural discourse, both the sixth- and seventh-cycle juries were concerned with 'universal relevance and contribution to the architectural and the social discourse of the world'. The distinction between the architectural and social discourse is important. In the realm of the architecture of buildings, the models of the Western world continue to dominate the major issues of architecture in the developing world. Buildings designed by Western or, in some cases, Japanese architects continue to be iconic models for most architects in the rest of the world. On occasions when the Islamic world offers its territory for the creation of world-class architecture, an architect from the West has been commissioned to build for the benefit of Islamic or secular societies within the context of the Islamic world. This year the jury clearly took a position that world-class buildings responding to the problems of change in the Islamic world had yet to emerge. In considering architectural projects, therefore, the jury clearly intended to imply that the importance of the buildings, of which there are five, was regional. In other words, the jury was not attempting to place buildings of excellence in a regional context into a global context. It was not searching for pluralistic or 'third way' messages to tie together regional architectural activities. On the contrary, the citation of these five buildings implies that their significance was confined to their regional context, a context within which their excellence should be judged. The jury had split its search into two categories. One category had importance within the territories that form the constituency of the Award; the other with 'recognizing projects that had a wider global context and meaning'.

The two projects 'seen to have qualities that could be of relevance to a broader global context' were essentially concerned with the reclamation of community space. These are projects of state patronage, removed from the world of international finance and essentially concerned with social issues. They have global significance because they are concerned with issues related to the reformulation of communities within the increasingly archaic nation-state.

In awarding these two projects for their broader universal values, the jury acknowledged the need for architecture to address the questions of community-based egalitarian futures. By recognizing the community as the accelerator of change in architecture, the Award is drawing attention to a contemporary architectural activity that the transatlantic architectural debates have long forgotten. Therefore, the message is not a pluralistic third way. It is a dualistic message that implies that the universal concerns of architecture are its social concerns, which must be clearly distinguished from regional architectural aspirations.

Both the Rehabilitation of Hebron Old Town and the Slum Networking of Indore City transcend their local contexts to generate solutions that have important symbolic

Rehabilitation of Hebron Old Town

values. Where, for instance, a designer or institutional catalyst substantially involves a local community and transforms with its help a deteriorating slum environment into a beautiful space, the practice of architecture also becomes a social or ideological act. More importantly, such work begins to redefine a significant symbolic role for architects as critical components in the reconstruction of community futures. When one considers the enormous damage done to the urban communities of Europe, in the former Yugoslavia or Northern Ireland, or considers the growing demands for the recognition of community identities such as those of the Basques, one also realizes that there is no other way to reconstruct these communities without the intense involvement of professional people who act as accelerators in the process of revitalizing communities in conflict. It is difficult to visualize other significant ways in which the growing homeless and jobless populations can be given futures in both the developed and underdeveloped parts of the world. Projects with a predominantly social content and in which degraded environments are transformed for the benefit of the poor and the outcast are crucial architectural achievements. The heroic role of architects and voluntary agencies in improving environments through a collaborative design process needs acclamation and serves as a reminder of the broader role that architecture has to play in the development process of all societies.

In rewarding such projects as Khuda-ki-Basti in Hyderabad in 1995 and the Hebron and Indore projects in 1998, the Award continues to emphasize that the universal message is a symbolic one that relates to bringing communities together. Because community conflicts are increasing rather than decreasing in all parts of the globe, the symbolic significance of the social projects transcends regional and national contexts. The model of the Grameen Bank Housing Programme awarded in the fourth cycle is much more important as a global model than an individual building placed within a regional context and commended for its architectural merit. The universal message of the Award is therefore contained in the recognition of these social projects. These can be regarded as symbols of hope in a world in which the structures and boundaries of nation-states that are being reformulated around communities with narrower cultural identities will become the building blocks of regions in the coming millennium.

# Continuity in a Changing Tradition

With respect to the issue of formulating a theory of tradition, Karl Popper raises two important questions: first, how does tradition arise and persist? and second, is the function of tradition in social life amenable to analysis?[1] Popper argues that tradition arises because of our need for a certain predictability in social life. In this sense, tradition provides order and regularity in our natural and social environment; it provides us with a 'means of communication' and a set of 'conventional usages and ideas' upon which we operate. Thus, the function of tradition is 'explanation and prediction'[2] and our need for structure and regularity in social life sustains it.

Popper draws an analogy between the role of tradition in society and the practical function of myths and theories in science. 'Scientific theories,' he states, 'are instruments by which we try to bring some order into the chaos in which we live so as to make it rationally predictable.' Similarly, the rise of 'traditions, like so much of our legislation, has just the same function of bringing some order and rational predictability into the social world in which we live.' The analogy goes further in suggesting that, since the significance of myths and theories in scientific thought lies in the idea that 'they [can] become the object of criticism, and … [can] be changed,' so too do 'traditions have the important double function of not only creating a certain order or something like a social structure, but also giving us something upon which we can operate, something we can criticise and change.'[3]

Given that the term 'tradition' contains a strong allusion to imitation, how can it be that tradition changes? And insofar as it does, can we continue to see it as one and the same tradition? In other words, is there what we might term 'continuity' in a changing tradition? And if so, which is more important for a society: the preservation of its tradition or the establishment of a sense of continuity with that tradition?

In dealing with this question, J.G.A. Pocock argues that, consciously or not, societies are organized to ensure their own continuity and thereby serve the function of preserving something from the past. Society's 'awareness of the past is in fact society's awareness of its continuity.'[4] Pocock sees society's own structure as the single most important element of continuity between its past and its present; thus, societies often conceive of their past in a way that ensures the continuity of their structure. He shows that a society may have as many pasts and modes of dependence on those pasts as it has past-relationships[5] and that it may also have as many pasts and relationships with those pasts as it has elements of continuity. Believing that a sense of continuity with the past arises from the working of social institutions, Pocock advocates the use of law rather than narrative history as a means of studying the past; in this way, he argues, one can determine from the legal record a description of the way in which these social institutions have worked.[6]

# Saleh Al–Hathloul

## Tradition and Continuity

In order to define and deal with the problem of tradition, let us examine, in the context of the development of the *shari'ah* (the Islamic legal tradition) during the second and third centuries AH (eighth and ninth AD), both the idea of tradition as something upon which we can operate (that is, a tradition which is constantly modified) and the concept of 'continuity within a changing tradition'.[7]

The development of the early schools of law at Kufah and Medina (subsequently known as the Hanafi and Maliki schools respectively) began in the early decades of the second century AH (first half of the eighth century AD). The schools developed as a result of the need to re-evaluate the legal practices that had arisen during the Umayyad period. Umayyad judges faced overwhelming problems owing to the enormously rapid expansion of Muslim territories; thus, they tended to be somewhat pragmatic in implementing the spirit of the original laws of Islam as propounded by the Qur'an. The schools began with the review of various local practices, legal and popular, in light of Islam's original aims and objectives. Gradually, a body of Islamic doctrine developed in the form of two schools.[8] Institutions and activities were individually considered in light of the principles of conduct enshrined in the Qur'an. These were then approved or rejected according to whether they met or fell short of these criteria. The process originated in the personal reasoning, or *ra'y*, of individual scholars and developed into a consensus of opinion of a given school's jurists. This subsequently became the idea of the *sunnah*. *Sunnah* originally meant actual customary practice, but in second-century AH (eighth AD) jurisprudence, it came to have a different connotation. For the scholars of the time, *sunnah* was 'the ideal doctrine established in the school and expounded by its current representatives'.[9] To understand how the consolidation of tradition through the establishment of continuity worked in the development of the Islamic legal system, an awareness of the changing connotation of the word *sunnah* during the development of the *shari'ah* is essential.

In the early 'Abbasid period, legal and political aspirations were to revive the purity of Islam during its Medina period. This could be achieved only by cutting through the Umayyad period and representing legal doctrine as having its roots in the earliest days. Thus, jurists attempted to establish a sense of continuity with the time of the 'rightly guided' rulers *(alkhulafa' alrashidun)*. This was achieved in two ways: first, in the interest of the consistency and coherence of the doctrine, reasoning was made more systematic, so that the personal *ra'y* gradually gave way to *qiyas* or analogical deduction. Second, emphasis on the notion of *sunnah*, or the established doctrine of a school, began to grow to reflect each school's purported continuity with the original tradition. As N.J. Coulson puts it, 'In order to consolidate the idea of tradition, the doctrine was represented as having roots stretching back into the past and the authority of previous generations was claimed for its current expression.'[10] This process was projected backwards to the early generations of Muslims, culminating with the Prophet himself as the authority for the doctrine.

By the middle of the second century AH (around 770 AD), the generally accepted legal methods of the early schools were challenged. The opposition adopted a doctrinaire attitude towards the substance of the law and its basis in jurisprudence, and claimed that the tendency of the early schools to project the *sunnah* backwards into the past did not go far enough. They saw the precedent of the Prophet himself as the supreme and overriding authority for law, and thus heightened the potential conflict of principle between the authority of the Prophet seen through *hadith* (or a precedent set by the Prophet) and the contemporary consensus of opinion among the local scholars as reflected by the *sunnah*. As a result of this potential conflict, the doctrine of the early schools was gradually modified to acknowledge some of the stricter rules advanced by the opposition and the growing tendency to claim the authority of the Prophet for the doctrine and to express it in the form of *hadith*.

In effect, legal development in this period was marked by the increasing diversity of doctrine. The opposition's challenge to the establishment in the early schools had now crystallized into a conflict of principles. The issue was polarized: should jurists maintain the right to reason for themselves as advocated by the establishment (*ahl al-ra'y*) or should they accept the exclusive authority of precedents from the Prophet as advocated by the doctrinaire opposition *(ahl al-hadith)*? To use Pocock's terms, 'a problem in past-relationships' had arisen, and some unifying process was necessary in order to establish 'notes of continuity' and to save the law from total disintegration.

This process was undertaken by al-Shafi'i (d. 204 AH, or 820 AD), whose main purpose was the unification of the law. To re-establish tradition and to imbue a sense of continuity in the law, al-Shafi'i recognized *sunnah* as a second source of law after the Qur'an. For al-Shafi'i, *sunnah* was the divinely inspired behaviour of the Prophet, while in the early schools it signified the local tradition of the individual school. By replacing the schools' concept with one originating from a single source, that is, the actions of the Prophet himself, al-Shafi'i hoped to eliminate a root cause of diversity between the different schools and to give uniformity to the doctrine. Two additional sources of the law were recognized by al-Shafi'i's theory: *ijma'*, or consensus, and *qiyas*, or reasoning by analogy. Both notions already existed, but al-Shafi'i gave them new connotations designed to achieve uniformity in the law. For *ijma'*, al-Shafi'i argued that the only valid consensus was that of the entire Muslim community, not simply the agreement of scholars in a given locality.[11] For *qiyas*, al-Shafi'i repudiated the undisciplined forms of reasoning such as *ra'y* or *istihsan* and insisted on the exclusive validity of strictly regulated analogical reasoning. Thus, al-Shafi'i achieved his goals not by introducing new concepts but by 'giving existing ideas a new orientation, emphasis and balance'.[12] His contribution lies in bringing these ideas together for the first time to form a systematic scheme of what would become known as the 'roots of law' [*usul al-fiqh*].[13]

Al-Shafi'i's position on the *sunnah* as the divinely inspired behaviour of the Prophet proved irrefutable and was therefore gradually accepted. From then on, the *hadith*, or precedents of the Prophet, could no longer be rejected through the objective criticism of their contents. The authority of the *hadith* was now considered binding, and the only possibility for criticism was to deny the authenticity of the oral accounts. As a result of the Shafi'i thesis, a new science of the Prophet's tradition, *'ilm al-hadith*,[14] developed, and three more schools of law were formed: one followed al-Shafi'i's own teaching and was named for him; the others, the Hanbali and Zahiri schools, were extreme supporters of tradition. The earlier Hanifi and Maliki schools adopted a more reserved attitude towards al-Shafi'i's thesis. Since strict adherence to his thesis would have required a complete revision of their existing *corpus juris*, they accepted the authority of the *sunnah* of the Prophet in a qualified form.[15] The adjustment process was undertaken without much difficulty because most of the doctrine of the two early schools was already expressed in the form of Prophetic *hadith* and precedents.

The classical theory of Islamic law developed during the third century AH (ninth AD) after al-Shafi'i's death. Though it comprises the *usal*, or sources, laid down by al-Shafi'i – the Qur'an, *sunnah*, *qiyas* and *ijma'* – its composite structure is fundamentally different. It aims at reasserting and preserving the Islamic legal tradition as developed up to that point. At the time, *ijma'* was accepted as the agreement of the acknowledged jurists in a given generation and was considered binding for later generations. *Ijma'* therefore provided for and tolerated the variations adopted by the different schools of law that al-Shafi'i had tried to eliminate. In classical theory, *ijma'* becomes 'the self-asserted hypothesis of Muslim jurisprudence'[16]; it is a material source of law in itself. For al-Shafi'i, it held a minor and trivial role owing to the near impossibility of consensus of the whole Muslim community. In the new classical theory, *ijma'* guaranteed the authenticity of the Qur'an and the *sunnah* as records of divine revelation, and the validity of *qiyas*. Most of all it guaranteed the authority of the whole structure of the legal theory. As soon as this *ijma'* was accepted, *ijtihad*, that is, independent judgment, eventually disappeared and the process of theoretical legal development in Islam finally ended with *ijma'*.

Throughout the development of the *shari'ah,* the desire was always to reaffirm the past as a valid guide to the present. Thus the *shari'ah* was advanced, accepted and took the shape of a tradition. This tradition was subjected to evaluation, criticism and change throughout the second and third centuries of Islam, until, for reasons too complex and controversial for consideration here, it came to a halt.[17] What is relevant here is that when its theoretical development stopped, the *shari'ah* as a tradition was not challenged. Whatever problems arose, they were considered manageable, and the tradition was accepted by both the jurists and the Muslim community without being questioned. Pocock's questions, why should the present follow the past? and how did the past become the present?, never arose. The tradition was accepted; it was assumed that the present was not different from the past.

## Urban Tradition

The pattern of a dominant, unchallenged and long-standing tradition was repeated in the physical environment of Muslim cities. Within this environment, a certain building tradition was developed and accepted. This tradition was no doubt evaluated, criticized and probably changed, but a sense of continuity persisted. With the beginning of the twentieth century AD, however, this tradition was challenged. An orthogonal street grid, new building types, such as the detached house (the villa) and the apartment building, and new materials like reinforced concrete, cement block and glass began to replace the winding street patterns, the attached houses with courtyards and the mud, stone and wooden materials that were the basic components of traditional urban forms in Muslim cities. As a result, a physical environment that is markedly different from the traditional one was introduced. The present now differed sharply from the past; thus, Pocock's question of how the present came to be what it is requires an answer.[18] However, my concern here is to reinterpret the past in a way that is useful and suitable for the present: that is, in a way that will re-establish a sense of continuity and eliminate the rupture and sense of alienation being voiced as a result of the introduction of a contemporary environment.[19] Since this concern implies that the past has a certain value for the present, the question whether the present should follow the past needs to be addressed.

Two responses to this question have been advocated in the Islamic world.[20] First, traditionalists simply reaffirm the validity of the past as a guide to the present, removing themselves from the difficult situation of the present and accepting the authority of the past as the only source for the present. By its very nature, this position does not allow for innovation and change, and therefore can produce only traditionalism.[21] Liberals, on the other hand, accept neither the authority nor the authenticity of the past as a source for the present. Their position, as Abdullah Laroui analyzes it, is based on the assumption that 'tradition is a destiny' and 'progress is necessarily an intervention from outside'.[22]

This position denies a given society's freedom of choice and implies a lack of authenticity and non-participation on the part of a traditional culture and population. It also implies that certain cultures are inferior to others. The result is a desire on the part of liberals to wipe away everything and start from scratch or, as Popper puts it, 'to clean the canvas'[23] and to import as many ideas and materials as possible from presumably superior cultures.[24] Both positions remove themselves from the present, the traditionalists by withdrawing backwards in time, and the liberals by moving elsewhere in place; neither seems to be actually dealing with the problems of the present.

I want to advocate a position that takes an interest in the present. It does not blindly accept the authority of the past, although it recognizes its authenticity and therefore its value as a resource for the present. It sees the liberal position, which denies the importance and influence of tradition, as futile. As Popper writes, 'You may create a new theory, but the new theory is created in order to solve those problems which the old theory did not solve'.[25] Thus, one cannot discard the old theory as if it never existed. In the same sense, one cannot accept the traditionalist position that sanctifies anything from the past. Tradition *per se* should have no authority but it does have value, for it forms the most important source of our knowledge and serves as the base for our thoughts and actions; in other words, tradition is a *platform* upon which one can operate. This tradition must be open to evaluation and criticism. As Stanford Anderson writes, 'The tradition we prize is not a mere accumulation of knowledge, an undifferentiated catalogue of past events, but rather a vital body of ideas, values, mores and so forth that we have as yet found resistant to criticism.'[26] In this sense, tradition becomes a choice rather than a destiny.

Our problem today, as alluded to earlier, is that physical environments in modern Muslim cities are totally different from traditional ones. This has resulted in a sense of discontinuity and alienation for the inhabitants. How did this come about and how can we re-establish a sense of urban continuity with the past?

In order to study both past and present physical environments and to investigate Muslim society's awareness of its past, we should direct our attention to the present activities and institutions that give rise to an awareness of the past and to the modes of awareness they produce. In this regard, the law as a highly institutionalized form represents a valuable asset, especially in a Muslim society where the *shari'ah* regulates all aspects of life and provides behavioural rules of conduct. As forms of convention, legal decisions represent an important, if not the most important, part of the entire social fabric. Their role is more powerful and significant than that of any other social institution because they make a genuine connection between the physical and the social fabric.

They provide us with the body of information necessary to investigate the relationship between political, sociocultural and environmental factors.

In order to understand how the physical environment of the Muslim city came about, one can look at it as a 'whole' and attempt to provide an interpretation of urban forms through their historical and cultural contexts. We will not deal with elements of urban forms, but look at the forms themselves as part of a broader Islamic tradition. These forms are seen as the physical environment in which the sociocultural and religious Muslim institutions developed and grew. The emphasis will be on why these physical forms took their existing and distinctive shape, rather than looking at the shape itself, for an interpretation. The next step will be to look at their process of formation and how different elements were used to create the distinctive physical environment that is looked upon as unique to the Muslim tradition. We will examine one theme, the concern for privacy, to see how it affected urban forms within the city and the house in particular. We will show how legal decisions regarding the specific problems of use and urban forms led to a certain shape for the Muslim house.

## The Architecture of the Muslim House

Given the intensely close family life and strict code of conduct for Muslims, it is not unusual for the issue of privacy to come under the purview of jurists. To be able to see into a house more than what a passer-by on the street would see is looked upon as an intrusion into the private life of the household. Such an act is considered to cause great harm and damage, and Muslim law has always insisted on the removal of damage. The concern for privacy is reflected in the physical forms of the traditional Muslim house in several ways, including the placement of doors, the architectural treatment of windows and the limit on building heights throughout the city.

The Maliki scholars did not allow a door to open in front of or near another door. The reason, given by Ibn Al-Qasim (d. 191 AH, or 807 AD), was that the neighbour who owns the existing door has the right to say, 'I benefit from the place in front of my door in which you want to open yours. I open my door with no one intervening on my privacy, and I bring my loads near my door without causing inconvenience to anyone. Thus, I wouldn't let you open a door in front of mine or near to it since you may use it as a reception and entertainment area or for comparable matters.' However, on a thoroughfare, Ibn Al-Qasim allowed the owner to open his door wherever he wished.[27] Malik (d. 178 AH, or 795 AD), on the other hand, did not allow this. When asked about a thoroughfare on which an individual wanted to open a door across from an existing one, Malik replied, 'If this causes harm such as that in entering or exiting [from the new door] he can see what is behind the [existing] door, then he should be prevented from opening it.'[28] Sahaun (d. 239 AH, or 854 AD) went further, to say that 'one must place his door at least one or two cubits from the facing door', even on a large, through street.[29]

Restrictions on building heights *per se* did not prevail in Muslim cities. When the famous general Khalid B. Al-Walid complained to the Prophet that his house on the eastern side of the Prophet's mosque was too small to accommodate his family, the Prophet replied, 'Build higher in the sky and ask God for spaciousness'.[30] However, damage caused by raising a building was not tolerated by the jurists. When asked whether an individual could raise his house higher than his neighbour's (and thus be able to look into the neighbour's house), Ibn Al-Qasim said, 'One has the right to raise his edifice, but I heard Malik say that he should be prevented from inflicting damage.'[31] Intrusion into the private life of the residents is considered to be a great damage, and if the placement of doors opposite each other was considered an intolerable intrusion, then obviously neighbours would not tolerate being under the constant view of others, either from open windows or from rooftops.

Ibn Al-Qasim was also asked about an individual who opened a door or a window in his own wall, from which he looked upon his neighbour and intruded upon his privacy. Relating his decision to Malik, he stated, 'One has no right to create something that will inflict harm or damage to his neighbour, even when what is done is within his own property.'[32] Other Maliki scholars would not tolerate the infliction of damage, even if the source predated the object on which the damage was now being inflicted.

At a later time, Ibn Al-Rami (d. 134 AH, or 1334 AD), when speaking of doors and windows that looked upon neighbouring houses, stated that in Tunis, 'The customary judgment as well as the usual practice is to prevent intruding and uncovering. This was the opinion of the judge Ibn 'Abd Al Rafi' (d. 133 AH, or 1333 AD), who in many cases which occurred during his time, ordered [the windows] to be sealed.'[33] At a later time, in a case from Medina (980 AH, or 1573 AD), an individual sued his neighbour in court for opening windows in his upper chamber, claiming that the open windows denied him privacy within his own house and thus caused him damage. After investigating the case and being assured that damage was being inflicted, the judge ordered the windows to be sealed, so the damage to the neighbour was removed.[34]

The other intrusion into neighbouring houses is the use of the rooftop. Since most Arab Muslim cities are in arid climates, roofs are usually used for living and sleeping on summer nights because large open yards rarely exist within urban dwellings. Related to this, we have the opinion of Sahnun in a case regarding the use of the rooftop of a mosque overlooking other houses. He emphasized that a protecting wall must be

ABOVE A typical Medina courtyard house.

BELOW The *qa'a* house has a small covered courtyard called a *qa'a* at its centre.

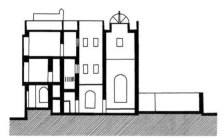

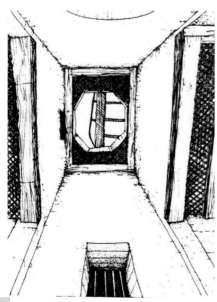

built and that no one could pray there before it was walled. At a later time, Ibn Al-Rami related a case that took place in Tunis where an individual had a staircase to his roof. Both the staircase and the roof were protected by a wall. The wall fell down and therefore anyone ascending to the roof was able to see into the neighbouring house. The neighbour asked the owner to rebuild the protecting wall, but he refused and was therefore sued in court. The judge did not compel the owner to rebuild the wall but made him liable to punishment should he or anyone else ascend to the roof.[35] The liability of punishment here is significant because it indicates the seriousness of the violation in the eyes both of the jurists and the citizens.

In the jurists' opinions for cases in Medina and Tunis, there is a highly institutionalized social context. Several levels are at work in these documents: first, actual building forms; second, social conflict; third, a regulatory mechanism, the court, which relies on precedent; and, fourth, the ideal system, in this case Islam, within which these conventions were moulded and can be transformed when the need arises.

Thus, one can say that the architecture of the Muslim house was to a great extent shaped by the *shari'ah* plus social conventions. In the placement of doors, the opening of windows, the height of a building and the treatment of the roof, there have always been rules for producing appropriate forms. These rules can be seen as 'the deep structure' or 'system of arrangement' that held the different elements together. This system can be seen in the houses in Medina. The house type in Medina was originally the courtyard house, typical of other Muslim cities. In later times, two other types emerged: the *qa'a* house and the *mashrabiyya* house.

The *qa'a* house contains a covered, small courtyard, called a *qa'a,* at its centre. The *qa'a,* used as the main reception room, is usually divided into three parts. The central part rises to the roof, where there is a removable cover; the two side parts have a lower roof with one or more floors above them. The *mashrabiyya* house, in its simplest form, is a typical row house with windows to the street covered with *mashrabiyyas* and, on the opposite side, high openings that allow for ventilation and daylight but do not give a view on to other houses. This type is usually four to five storeys, while the courtyard house rarely exceeds two floors. The *qa'a* type is generally two or three floors.

The sequence in which the three house types emerged in Medina is believed to be: first, the courtyard type; second, the *qa'a;* and last, the *mashrabiyya* type. The two latter types provided a substitute for the courtyard type. The changes occurred when the prevailing conditions either did not permit the preceding type or that type was no longer feasible owing to high land prices that required a more efficient building. The eighteenth-century development of the *mashrabiyya* house along the *sahah* (the main street leading from the *shami* gate to the Mosque of the Prophet), for example, occurred

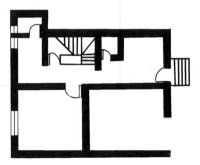

The *mashrabiyya* house is a typical terraced house with covered windows on the street side and no courtyard.

when the economic value of the area rose because of the proximity of the mosque. In spite of changes in form, however, each new type subscribed to the system of arrangement, or legal system, for forms in the city.

## Continuity in the Contemporary Architecture of Saudi Arabia

The modernization process of the past thirty years has continued to challenge architectural tradition in Saudi Arabia with the introduction of new materials, techniques and systems. With the economic boom of the 1970s and early 1980s, many building programmes were launched, some of which neither took account of the natural and climatic conditions of the area nor responded to the sociocultural traditions of the people. Only in the 1980s did attempts by some Saudi architects to re-establish continuity with the past begin to emerge. These architects subscribed to the underlying structure of values, norms and conventions that govern social behaviour, and as long as this system is understood and provided for in design, the identity exists. In their quest for continuity, they followed two different approaches. Followers of one approach strongly believe in the need for a continuity of a style; adherents of the other subscribe to the idea that, as long as the main themes and principles are understood and provided for in the design, then the final architectural forms will satisfy.

For Qasr Al-Hokm District, an urban design study for the Riyadh city centre conceived in the early 1980s, the Beeah Group prepared a package consisting of building codes, development regulations, a land-use plan and an illustrative design scheme to show how the regulations could be applied and their possible outcome.[36] The project dealt with many issues including land tenure, land-use control and design guidelines, for which the designers looked at legal precedents in the Muslim world. Locating precedent for different land uses proved to be more complicated because the project included commercial, business, residential, cultural and religious activities. The cultural and religious activities were already fixed in the old city. For the commercial activities and the organization of markets, the designers evoked the main principles established by the jurists and stated in *hisbah* manuals for organizing markets within the traditional Muslim city. In developing the urban design guidelines, the designers sought to understand the essence of the *shari'ah* law and how it was reflected in the built environment. Traditional regulations emanated from behavioural rules of conduct; thus, they were prospective in nature, specifying actions or behaviours that were allowed but leaving the door open for creativity. Regulations today are prescriptive in nature, specifying what is allowed and how it is to be done, thus narrowing design options and limiting creativity.

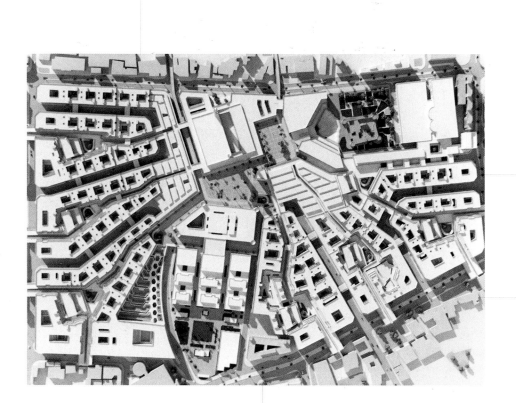

The proposal for the Qasr Al-Hokm district by the Beeah Group.

Existing building codes in Riyadh mandate certain building setbacks and allow second-floor openings that overlook neighbouring houses. People have reacted to the latter in two ways. Either they go to court and sue their neighbours, or they protect themselves by extending their fences with plastic corrugated sheets. To avoid this contradiction between existing regulations and clearly strong social values, the Beeah Group did not allow openings that overlook adjacent or lower dwelling units. Telling designers what is not allowed, rather than what is allowed, gives them the flexibility to develop different and perhaps innovative solutions. In one scheme, this issue was solved by opening windows on to terraces and courtyards with high parapets, and by using high windows that admit daylight but avoid views on to adjacent dwellings and skylights, in essence, a modified form of the *qa'a*.

The design guidelines also consider identity. People usually become more conscious of a tradition when they begin to lose it. The Beeah Group looked at the basic principles and values of the past to ascertain whether they were still viable and, if so, to revive and develop them, such as the principle of privacy. It was also felt that the project should maintain the indigenous architectural style of the region in order to preserve the identity of the old city of Riyadh. Criteria were developed to make this decision sufficiently flexible and to ensure that traditional themes would be used in a contemporary way.[37]

In 1985, in order to produce distinctive prototypical residential units, the Riyadh Municipality commissioned several architectural firms to design sixteen prototypical units on lots of 20 x 25 metres and located along streets 15 to 25 metres wide. Aware of the sociocultural traditions and environmental conditions of Riyadh, the designers approached the Municipal Houses Prototype, or El-Naim, starting with a review of existing codes and regulations, such as the allowance for window openings on all sides, which overlook outside spaces in neighbouring dwellings. This, the designers concluded, contradicted existing values, norms and social conventions, as well as the climatic and environmental conditions of the hot, arid region, and they went back to study traditional environments. The traditional house type in Riyadh was the courtyard house, but to design around a courtyard and meet the present-day setback requirements

would waste space and not provide privacy. Thus the designers established three principles as a basis for rewriting the regulations: efficient and full use of all spaces; protection of inhabitants' privacy; and a more responsive microclimate within each dwelling unit. This led them to abolish the mandatory setback requirements, to prohibit windows that overlook interior or exterior spaces in neighbouring houses and to use the courtyard as a design feature.

In the final design, care was taken to reduce the surfaces directly exposed to the sun by abolishing setbacks and creating a system of courtyards that created an appropriate climate within each dwelling. The privacy of the inhabitants was achieved by directing all windows and openings towards courtyards, terraces and roofs with parapets. Windows were not allowed to be opened in the outside wall.[38]

The designers of the municipal houses did not opt for a specific architectural character or style. They believed that as long as sociocultural values and environmental conditions were understood and provided for in the design, then the resulting forms would preserve identity and produce a feeling of continuity.

ABOVE A view of the central section of the Qasr Al-Hokm proposal, showing the architectural language employed in the design.

BELOW A model of the Municpal Houses Prototype in Riyadh shows 20 x 25 metre lots, highlighting the relationship between built and open space.

The existing regulations for building in Riyadh – requiring setbacks and allowing window openings that overlook neighbouring dwellings – represent the liberals' position that progress is an intervention that should come from outside the society. Whether consciously or not, they desire to wipe away traditional norms and conventions. The Beeah Group and El-Naim designers recognize the need to re-establish continuity with the past. As a result of their research of the past, they believe in the value of tradition as a resource and a platform upon which one can operate. They believe in Popper's proposition that it is possible to create a new theory in order to solve the problems that the old theory did not solve, rather than discarding the old theory as if it never existed.

## Notes

1   Karl Popper, 'Towards a Rational Theory of Tradition', in his *Conjectures and Refutations : The Growth of Scientific Knowledge* (New York: Harper and Row, 1968),131.

2   These are Stanford Anderson's rephrasings of Popper. Stanford Anderson, 'Architecture and Tradition that isn't "Trad, Dad"', in M. Whiffen (ed.), *The History, Theory and Criticism of Architecture* (Cambridge Mass.: M.I.T. Press, 1970), 81-82.

3   Popper, op.cit., 131.

4   J.G.A. Pocock, 'The Origins of Study of the Past: A Comparative Approach,' in *Comparative Studies in Society and History*, 4 (1961-62), 209-246.

5   'Past relationship expresses the specialized dependence of an organized group or activity within society on a past conceived in order to ensure its continuity.' Ibid., 213.

6   Ibid., 243.

7   This is a brief sketch of the development of Islamic legal tradition that emphasizes the *Sunni* schools of law and the development of the structure of the law with an emphasis on looking to the past to proclaim the continuity of a present or promoted tradition with that of the past. This account is based mainly on three sources: N.J. Coulson, *A History of Islamic Law* (Edinburgh: Edinburgh University Press, 1964); S. Mahmassani, *Falsaft al-Tashri' fi al-Islam (The Philosophy of Jurisprudence in Islam)*, trans. F.J. Ziadeh (Leiden, 1961);J. Schacht, *An Introduction to Islamic Law* (London: Oxford University Press, 1964).

8   The schools' common ground was the explicit provision of the Qur'an, the precedents of the Prophet and the early Caliphs. Their legal method was basically the same but the systems of law which the two

schools created from it differed, though these differences were mostly in the details of the law. See Coulson, op. cit., 47-50.

9   Ibid., 39.

10  Ibid., 40.

11  Al-Shafi'i's concept of *ijma'* here aims to the authority of the *sunnah* of the school or local consensus, thereby eliminating the diversity of law and enforcing his concept of *sunnah*.

12  Coulson, op. cit., 61.

13  For the essence of al-Shafi'i's legal theory in its maturity, see his *al-Risalah* (Cairo, 1895). Translated into English by M. Khaduri in his *Islamic Jurisprudence* (Baltimore, 1961).

14  This had a major impact on scholarly activities during the third century AH, or ninth century AD, when the *sunnah* of the Prophet became the focal point. One of the main features of this period was the growth of a separate science, *'ilm al-hadith*, with a literature of its own. Specialist scholars devoted themselves to the process of collecting, documenting and classifying the *hadith* and actions of the Prophet according to certain criteria developed for this purpose. As a result, several compilations were produced, such as that of al-Bukhari (d. 256 AH, or 870 AD). Muslim jurisprudence accepted as authentic the corpus of *hadith* resulting from the activities of specialist scholars during this period. Coulson, op. cit., 62-70.

15  Both schools were reluctant to accept the binding nature of a single or isolated *hadith (khabar al-wahid)* when it contradicted their established doctrine. And both preserved subsidiary principles of jurisprudence in order to be able to override that

of isolated *hadith*. The *Hanafis* maintained the validity of *istihsan* (preference) and the *Malikis* that of *ijma' ahl al-Madinah* (the consensus of Medina).Coulson, op. cit., 72.

16  'For although the validity of the principle is formally expressed in a tradition from the Prophet which states: "my community will never agree upon an error", it is the *ijma'* itself which guarantees the validity of the Tradition.' Coulson, op. cit., 77.

17  Some writers have suggested the Mongol invasions as a reason for such phenomena. Coulson shows that this phenomenon occurred some three centuries before the invasion, and suggests that it was probably the result not of external pressures but of internal ones. His reasoning is that the material sources of the divine will had been fully exploited by that time and that an exaggerated respect for the personalities of former jurists induced the belief that the work of interpretation and expansion had been exhaustively accomplished by scholars of peerless ability, and he links this to the spread of *ijma'*. Coulson, op. cit., 80-81.

18  An attempt in this direction can be found in S. Al-Hathloul, *The Arab-Muslim City* (Riyadh: Dar Al-Sahan, 1996).

19  This sense of alienation has been voiced by many writers in the field of Muslim cities and Islamic architecture. See, for example, H. Fathy, 'Planning and Building in the Arab Tradition: The Village Experiment of Gourna', in M. Berger (ed.), *The New Metropolis in the Arab World* (Cairo, 1974), 210-229; 'Constancy, Transposition and Change in the Arab City', in L.C.Brown (ed.), *From Medina to Metropolis* (Princeton, 1973), 319-333. Most of the issues related to this process of alienation and change in the Muslim city and architecture have been raised in the Aga Khan Award for Architecture seminars.

20  Q. Zurayq, in 'Our Position towards the Past', counts four directions: the traditionalist, the nationalist, the Marxist and what he termed the 'scientific approach'. This last approach, according to him, exists only in the minds of a very few, and he therefore hopes to see it develop in the Arab world. The traditionalist is encompassed within our own first classification; the nationalist advocate can be found on both sides of our classification, depending on his way of looking at the past; and the Marxist advocates can be seen as similar to the liberals' point of view illustrated here. See Q. Zurayq, *Nahn wa al-Tarikh* (Beirut, 1959), 25-45.

21  A representative example of the traditionalist way of thinking can be found in M. Bahi, *Al-Fikr al-Islami*

al-Hadith wa-silatuhbi-al Isti'mar al-Gharbi, 2nd edn (Cairo, 1959).

22  A. Laroui, *The Crisis of the Arab Intellectual, Traditionalism or Historicism?* (Berkeley: University of California Press, 1976), 42.

23  Popper, op. cit., 131.

24  A representative example of the liberals' way of thinking is to be found in H. Sa'b, *Tahdith al-Fikr al-'Arabi* (Beirut, 1970).

25  Popper, op. cit., 132.

26  S. Anderson, op. cit., 81-82.

27  Malik b. Anas, a*l-Mudawwanah*, 16 vols, Cairo (1323 AH, or 1905 AD), v. XIV, 237.

28  Ibn al-Rami, *Kitab al-I'lan bi-Ahkam al-Bunyan*, manuscript of Rabat, Dar Al-Khizanah Al-'Ammah, No. A802834, 34.

29  Ibn Al-Imam, Trans. Barbier, 'Des droits et obligations entre propriétaires d'héritages voisins', in Revue Algérienne et Tunisienne de Législation et de Jurisprudence, 1900 (I) and 1901 (II): I, 98.

30  Al-Samhudi Wafa', *Al-Wafa'*, 2 vols, 2nd edn (Beyrouth, 1971), vol. 2, 370.

31  Malik, op. cit., v. XIV, 232.

32  Ibid, v. XI, 37.

33  Ibn al-Rami, op. cit., 25-26.

34  Medina Court Records from 963 AH, or 1555 AD, to the present time, R. 6, v. I, Case No. 418, 229.

35  Ibn al-Rami, op. cit., 29.

36  Information and illustrations on this project can be found in A. Shuaibi and S. Al-Hathloul, 'The Justice Palace District, Riyadh', in *Continuity and Change: Design Strategies for Large-scale Urban Development* (Boston: the Aga Khan Program for Islamic Architecture), 37-48.

37  This study provided a base from which several projects have been launched in the district, such as: *Al-Mu'ajqliyah* development west of the mosque in the mid-1980s, the Great Mosque of Riyadh and Old City Centre Redevelopment including the Justice Palace in late 1980s and the Arriyadh Development Co. project now under construction on the western side of the district.

38  Although these prototypes were spatially well designed and respond to sociocultural values and environmental factors, they were proposed for the public to choose from, simply because they do not take setback requirements into consideration.

# Pragmatism and the Built Environment

Most of the Islamic world was colonized by European nations in the nineteenth and early twentieth centuries. These colonial states, with the exception of the Central Asian republics, became independent after World War II and, along with the few Islamic states that had remained independent, adopted welfare state or socialist 'models' on which to base the development of their own societies. These models, drawn from European and Soviet experiences, were intended to provide for the physical and social needs of the urban centres.

Both models failed to deliver, however, because they were not compatible with the political, social, economic, demographic and cultural realities of the societies to which they were applied. As a result, the urban environments in most Islamic countries have deteriorated; 'adhocism' has replaced policy; helplessness has led to corruption; formal sector planning cannot reach the poor, who increasingly depend on an informal sector for the fulfilment of their needs; and numerous innovative projects (often funded by donor agencies) that can bridge the gap between theory and reality cannot be transformed into effective national programmes.

The repercussions of the failures of these two models on the built environment are many. However, four issues are of primary importance because they are having an adverse effect on the built environment in most Islamic cities. These four issues are the absence of land protection; the increasing gap in housing supply and demand; the absence of transport- and cargo-related infrastructure; and environmentally unfriendly developer-built housing.

Almost all city governments in the Islamic world own land and many cities have master and/or land-use plans. However, these land-use plans are seldom followed, and a powerful politician-bureaucrat-developer nexus (formal and informal) makes it possible for land to be encroached upon or acquired illegally for inappropriate commercial purposes. This process causes environmental degradation, denies the city space for recreation, culture and infrastructure and makes a mockery of official planning. Obviously, something is wrong with the institutional arrangements for developing and implementing urban plans if they can be routinely violated.

Millions if not billions of dollars have been invested over the last four decades in building the 'capacity and capability' of urban development agencies in the Islamic world, but land-use violations continue to grow. Therefore, it is also obvious that the problem is a conceptual one and is not related to capacity and capability alone. It is also important to note that in many mega-cities, citizens' groups have started to put pressure on development agencies to follow their plans and have taken steps to protect land from encroachment.

In the housing arena, the supply-and-demand gap has increased. In many Islamic cities the formal sector caters to no more than 20 per cent of the housing demand. This

# Arif Hasan

supply-and-demand gap is met in three ways: (1) by the illegal occupation and subdivision of state land by informal developers; (2) by the informal subdivision of agricultural land on the city fringe, always in defiance of government regulations; and (3) by the densification of inner-city settlements. These processes are not supported or guided by any professional input and lead to badly planned, unserviced settlements that have no relationship to each city's larger master plan. Since many of these settlements do not have the security of tenure, they also create immense social and political problems for the city. The subdivision and sale of agricultural land for housing purposes in sensitive locations is also adversely affecting the ecology of the regions in which the cities are situated.

Many innovative projects have been developed over the last 25 years for the upgrading of informal settlements and for providing land to the urban poor at affordable prices. However, none of these programmes has been able to expand to such an extent that the growth of informal settlements could be at all curtailed. In fact, these programmes have shrunk considerably in the past decade.

In most of the larger Islamic cities, the informal development of housing described above has now been institutionalized, and its various actors have a well-established relationship with each other and with government officials. The official planning process cannot replace the work that the informal developers are carrying out, and experience tells us that government agencies do not have the knowledge of development procedures or the ability to deliver housing that is compatible with the sociology and economics of low-income groups.

Many populations of Islamic cities have tripled and quadrupled in the last five decades owing to rural-urban migration. As a result, the demand for transport, wholesaling, retailing, cargo handling and related facilities has multiplied proportionately. However, most of these cities have only catered to the needs of residential, retailing and formal industrial requirements. As a result, the other requirements have developed informally, often in the old city centres that constitute the historic urban fabric. Much of the economy of the cities is also of an informal nature, unattended to by planners, and this too has developed in the inner cities.

Because of these factors the old city centres and inner cities have developed severe environmental problems and the historic fabrics have been damaged to varying degrees. Attempts have been made to rehabilitate these fabrics but this work has seldom been viewed as a part of a larger city planning exercise that is linked to city-owned land, infrastructure and housing issues.

Finally, there is the issue of developer-built housing. In recent years, there has been a phenomenal increase in the urban middle and lower-middle classes in Islamic

The typical, environmentally unfriendly developer-built housing in urban centres has changed the appearance of cities into characterless urban spaces that do not reflect their individual locations.

cities. Large-scale housing projects have been developed by private-sector developers to cater to the housing needs of these classes. This housing and related commercial development is determining the built environment of many large cities. This is the new 'urban vernacular'. Much of it is of very poor architectural quality and badly built. In almost all cases, it creates a bad physical and social environment and is unrelated either to other neighbouring developments or to larger ecological issues. Often, it violates building regulations. Increasingly, apartment owners' associations are being created to negotiate with developers for a better product, for implementation of building by-laws and for subsequent maintenance of the housing developments. Where owners' associations have the support of local government, they are able to protect the environment and get a better deal. In most cases, however, local governments either openly support the developers or prefer not to involve themselves.

Pragmatism demands that the politicians, planners, professional institutions and academia accept the above-stated realities. These realities cannot be wished away and conventional planning has not developed the means to relate to them; thus it is necessary to support the 'good practices' in them and regulate the bad ones. To do this, it is necessary first to accept this approach and, second, to understand these processes and the relationships between their various actors.

It is also necessary to understand and deal with two new realities. First, a new generation of city dwellers has come of age. These are the children of the first generation of migrants. Unlike their parents, they are not pioneers but are searching for a new identity that relates to the city in which they live. If the city gives them this opportunity, then they lobby and work for the physical and social development of their neighbourhoods and take an interest in citywide development. If not, they search for a larger political identity that often conflicts with the immediate and long-term social, cultural and physical interests of their city.

The other new reality is related to the fact that almost all Islamic countries have liberalized their economies and have been subjected to structural readjustment. Essential services are being privatized, state land is being sold for revenue generation, investment for public housing has been reduced and there is pressure to do away with subsidies on land and social facilities. State agencies and politicians will thus obviously play a lesser role in the development and management of city functions in the future.

A new agenda is required to deal with the issues related to the built environment in Islamic cities. This agenda should set in motion a new process that over time will give citizens control of the physical city as well as of the institutions that plan, implement and maintain the city.

The essential components of such an agenda should be:

• All government agencies should publish a list of their real-estate assets (including land) along with their present and future land-use proposals. NGOs, citizens groups, neighbourhood associations and professional institutions should be encouraged to prevent misuse of these real-estate assets. The citizens' groups, supported by the real-estate land-use listings, should also lobby for a law that prevents land-use changes without public hearings.
• In the housing sector, rules and regulations for supporting and regulating the functioning of the informal sector and its actors should be developed and implemented. Their work should be seen as a part of a larger city plan.
• Space for the development and growth of a transport- and cargo-related infrastructure should be given priority, along with space for the functions of the informal sector. Inner-city rehabilitation and conservation should be seen as a part of this process. A steering committee of the representatives of the various interest groups should receive all plans at the conceptual stage and supervise their implementation. This process will promote appropriate planning and introduce much-needed transparency and accountability in planning and implementation.
• By-laws related to developer-built housing should be revised so as to make it difficult to build housing complexes that are not conducive to creating a suitable physical and social environment. It is also necessary to institutionalize the relationship between apartment owners'/purchasers' associations and developers to ensure that building regulations are not violated and that the complexes are fully completed.

What is being asked for in the above agenda is to understand, support and/or regulate what is already happening and what experience tells us cannot be replaced. It also calls for the creation of a 'space' for interaction between politicians, planners and people (communities, interest groups representing the formal and informal sectors). Once it is created, this space will have to be nurtured over many years and finally institutionalized. The creation of this space cannot be achieved simply by enacting a law, but adopting the above agenda can make a beginning.

In the initiation of this process, the architectural profession has a very important role to play. It alone can give design and technical advice to informal sector processes; relate urban infrastructure projects to social, aesthetic, and conservation issues; develop relevant by-laws and regulations (and lobby for their implementation) to produce environmentally friendly, developer-built housing; and create a link between its own work and that of other actors in the built environment drama. How the profession can do all this is a subject that needs to be discussed and debated.

Large cities in Islamic countries have expanded rapidly in the last fifty years, resulting in an unsatisfactory physical and social environment for urban dwellers.

# Recipients of the 1998

## Aga Khan Award for Architecture

### Rehabilitation of Hebron Old Town

### Slum Networking of Indore City, India

### Lepers Hospital, Chopda Taluka, India

## Salinger Residence, Selangor, Malaysia

## Tuwaiq Palace, Riyadh, Saudi Arabia

## Alhamra Arts Council, Lahore, Pakistan

## Vidhan Bhavan, Bhopal, India

# Rehabilitation of Hebron Old Town

Planner/Conservator: Engineering Office

1995 and ongoing

Hebron Old Town has four distinct areas,
three of which surround the historic Haram
of Abraham, seen here at the upper right.

# f the Hebron Rehabilitation Committee

Client: **Hebron Rehabilitation Committee**

For an ambitious, creative and resourceful rehabilitation project,
realized under the most difficult circumstances. Hebron (*Al-Khalil* in
Arabic) perpetuates a very long collective Palestinian memory, rooted
in religious beliefs and a rich cultural and multi-faith legacy. Like other
Palestinian cities, Hebron has suffered from the well-known ongoing
conflicts between two peoples equally attached to their respective
religious legacies. In spite of these conditions, the revitalization of
the city is mainly due to the Palestinian people. Many sensitive issues
had to be faced in this project: land, property, identity and cultural
and historical consciousness. These were handled in a very effective
manner without disturbing the social structure of the city or shifting
the ownership of buildings from the original inhabitants. In awarding
this project, the Jury recognizes the skills, the competence and the
courage of the community, as well as the architectural relevance
of its work and the promising future role of the rehabilitated city. In
addition, this approach is valid for urban situations in many other
parts of the world.

Hebron, an old and sacred town, is an important religious centre for Islam, Judaism and Christianity. Located along the pilgrimage route to Mecca and on the road that connects Damascus to Cairo, the city has a long and sometimes turbulent history. For Muslims, it is a sacred city because of the Haram built over Machpelah Cave, which contains the grave of the Prophet Abraham. The Haram also holds the graves of Sarah, Isaac, Rebecca, Jacob and Leah. The first building over Machpelah Cave, now replaced many times over, is said to have been built by King Herod in the first century BC.

Today, Hebron is a city of 126,000 that has grown far beyond its original, ancient site west of the Wadi al-Khalil (Valley of Hebron) and on to the slopes of the surrounding four mountains. The old town of Hebron, now to the southeast of the modern city, dates from the eighteenth century. It consists of four distinct areas, three of which surround the Haram of Abraham.

The rehabilitation and restoration of Hebron Old Town essentially began in 1988 with the initiation of the Hebron University Graduates Union (UGU), a group concerned with the old urban fabric of the city and the buildings that constituted it. Before the Israeli presence in Hebron began in 1967, the population of the old town was 10,000, but the ensuing conflicts led to an evacuation of the area, and 85 per cent of the historic stone houses were abandoned. These large, extended-family houses, called *hosh*, are thick-walled stone structures, generally two and three storeys high and asymmetrically clustered around a courtyard. Left empty and unattended, the buildings fell into disrepair, thus leaving the core of the old city in decline. Between 1988 and 1991, the UGU conducted a comprehensive survey of the area and determined that many of the dwellings could still be saved and re-inhabited.

The UGU's work led to development of the Hebron Rehabilitation Committee (HRC), a thirteen-member group that includes government ministers and

**LEFT**  A minaret at the Haram of Abraham rises above the rehabilitated and re-inhabited clustered stone buildings in Hebron Old Town.

**ABOVE**  The rehabilitation of extended-family courtyard houses, called *hosh*, has been achieved without making overtly modern additions or major alterations to the historic structures. Many of the revitalized dwellings provide housing for low-income tenants.

BELOW A small souk lines one side of an open area where buildings were destroyed in the nineteenth century. Renovated dwellings now surround the space, which the Hebron Rehabilitation Committee plans to develop as a community park.

representatives of community NGOs, including the UGU. The executive branch of the HRC is the Engineering Office, which acts as the town planning office in Hebron. It assumed responsibility for a 'General Policy for Restoration', a document that addresses not only restoration guidelines for the historic houses but also the means of upgrading to make them habitable. Changes that would jeopardize the architectural and historical value of buildings are prohibited, yet such modern conveniences as kitchens, toilets and running water can be incorporated. The HRC employs a staff of thirty-two, and has hired eight consultants and twenty contracting services to work in the old town.

Work on the houses began in 1995 and will continue until 2002. To date, 127 dwellings and twenty-five shops have been restored, and work is presently going on in ninety-five other buildings. Only the minimum work necessary is being done. For example, no extensive reconstruction

LEFT (from far left) Despite the deterioration caused by neglect, most of the buildings did not suffer from major structural problems. A minimal amount of work was necessary to make them sound and functional, as seen in these pairs of before and after photographs.

BELOW The existing and proposed urban profile of Hebron Old Town, prepared by the Engineering Office overseeing the rehabilitation work.

■ Rehabilitated Area

■ Ongoing Rehabilitation

■ Documented

□ Ongoing Documentation

▨ Future Projects

□ Israeli Settlers

REHABILITATION OF HEBRON OLD TOWN

**ABOVE** Saving the old town buildings preserves the historic legacy of Hebron. Every building must be documented by drawings, reports and photographs before the work commences, and no radical changes are permitted to the exterior. The primary material used in the renovation work is concrete, but all exterior surfaces are clad in stone. As many as 20 different contractors are working in the old town to save the old buildings.

is undertaken to complete missing parts of buildings. The primary interventions are the provision of stairs where needed, the addition of running water, which includes all necessary piping for sewage, and new electric wiring. Alterations are limited primarily to the interiors in order to preserve the historical value of the visible urban fabric. Only the door and window openings, originally made in wood, have been changed, refitted with metal frames, grilles and shutters for safety reasons.

**RIGHT** The building stock of Hebron Old Town has survived more than one period of construction, but it is generally accepted that most date from the eighteenth century.

**BELOW** The open area on top of most houses is closed in by a parapet wall, which was originally topped by a band of equilateral triangles composed of terracotta tubes, called *kizan*, embedded in lime mortar. In summer the *kizan* were filled with water to cool the air passing through them, making the rooftop terrace more pleasant.

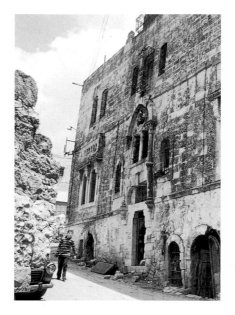

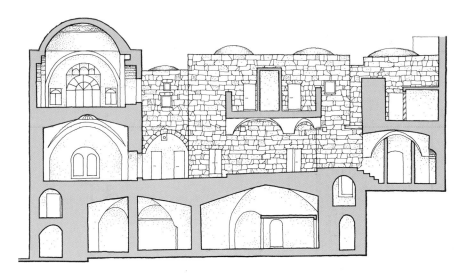

BELOW and RIGHT Local stone and lime mortar are used to fill small cracks in the walls. If a large structural crack is found, the wall is taken down and rebuilt to resemble the original. Roofs and domes are resealed with concrete and re-insulated in either light beige or dark grey materials.

The revitalization of Hebron Old Town is financed through public and international funding. To date, the Hebron Rehabilitation Committee estimates that it has spent US $3,000,000. The cost of rehabilitating one house is about US $200 per square metre. As buildings have been completed, families have moved back to the old town. By 1997, the population of Hebron Old Town was 2,000.

Though the old town had been mostly abandoned for more than twenty years, the ownership of 99 per cent of the

structurally sound and comfortable without introducing a disturbing difference between the restored and unrestored buildings. Because of the pride and concern of the local community, the once nearly abandoned and dilapidated Hebron Old Town is now a healthy, living and vibrant part of the city.

**ABOVE** Residential rooms are typically small and square. The majority of living spaces are covered with star vaults, the centre of which is elaborated in a small cupola, while smaller rooms are cross-vaulted.

**OPPOSITE ABOVE** Renovating the old *hosh* for current and future use means introducing a kitchen where possible. The mosque supplied meals for the old town neighbourhood at the time when many of the houses were originally built, hence cooking rooms were not included.

**OPPOSITE** and **RIGHT** The rehabilitation plan also includes work on monuments in Hebron. The Turkish Bath has been restored for use as a museum (seen here) and work is being done to restore vault paintings and stone panels in the Abraham Mosque.

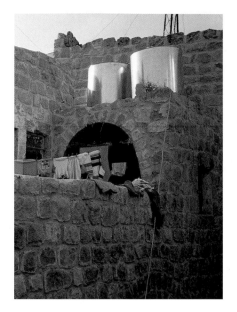

**ABOVE** and **LEFT** Children playing in *hosh* courtyards and laundry hanging out to dry on rooftops testify to a reinvigorated town. The roofs now also support large capacity water tanks for the newly plumbed dwellings. The stone-clad courtyards are decorated with garden plants in pots.

**OPPOSITE** Renovation work, including new frames for doorways and extensive repointing of the stone walls, is faithful to the original character of Hebron Old Town architecture.

# Slum Networking of Indore City

Planner: **Himanshu Parikh**, Civil Engineer

1989 and ongoing

Gandhinagar

Futi Kothi

In Indore, landscaped riverbanks now
overlook a clean river that was formerly
a sewage-filled, low-water river lined
with decrepit slums.

For having successfully mobilized and coordinated the financial
and human resources of funding agencies, government
organizations, NGOs and local communities in order to create a
better living environment for the residents of the informal settlements
of Indore and, in the process, reclaiming for public use the formerly
polluted lakes and riverfronts of the city. This has been done by
establishing an innovatively planned, low-cost, city-level sewerage
network, a solid-waste management system and recreational areas.
What is unique about the Slum Networking of Indore City is that
the slum regularization and upgrading exercise is part of a larger
environmental upgrading plan for the entire city. The application
of this approach to other similar conditions would go a long way
in overcoming the weaknesses of conventional urban upgrading
projects, which seldom attempt to integrate slums into the
urban fabric.

The Slum Networking of Indore City is a community-based sanitation and environmental improvement programme that regards urban slums not as resource-draining liabilities but as opportunities to make sustainable changes and improvements to the city as a whole. Devised and pioneered in the city of Indore by the engineer Himanshu Parikh, the networking concept was made possible and sustainable by bringing together communities, governments, NGOs and industry for its implementation.

Centrally located in India's fertile Malwa Plateau, midway between Delhi and Bombay, Indore is a marketing and distribution centre for cotton, nuts, wheat and other cash crops, as well as an important textile-manufacturing city. Its growth as a business and transport centre has created numerous employment opportunities, resulting in a continuing rural-urban migration of jobseekers. Most of these people move into the 183 slums that are scattered throughout the city, many of them on the banks of the Khan

and Saraswati rivers. Of Indore's total population of 1,400,000 (in 1995), 28 per cent live in slums, a proportion expected to rise to 30 per cent by 2000. The Muslim population constitutes 25 per cent of the inner city of Indore.

The Indore sewer system built in 1936 served only 5 per cent of the city's population. All the sewage and solid waste were discharged into the Khan and Saraswati rivers, which resulted in unhygienic conditions in the city and poor health in the slums. The concept of the networking project was to create an efficient urban infrastructure that in turn would help to upgrade the slums. Himanshu Parikh took advantage of the pattern of the Indore slums in order to introduce an efficient infrastructure path for sewage, storm drainage, and fresh water services that followed the natural river course. An extensive physical survey was conducted to plot the city's natural drainage paths to the river, and a socioeconomic survey identified the slum families with the greatest needs. The

ABOVE Secondary paths through the slums, once covered in mud, have been dramatically improved with the introduction of sewerage lines and concrete paving.

OPPOSITE Physical improvements made under the programme include paved roads and footpaths, storm drainage, water supply and sewerage hook-ups, street lighting, landscaping and solid waste management.

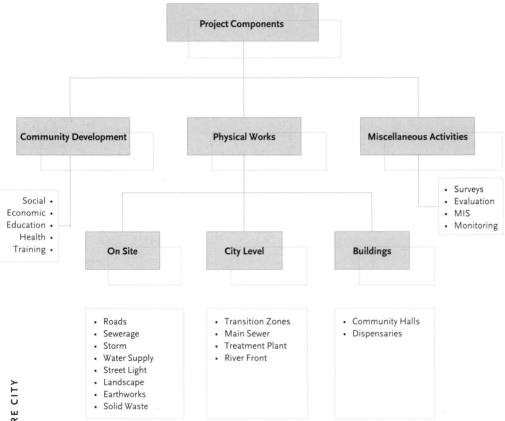

```
                    ┌─────────────────────┐
                    │  Project Components │
                    └─────────────────────┘
```

**Project Components**

**Community Development**

- Social
- Economic
- Education
- Health
- Training

**Physical Works**

**On Site**
- Roads
- Sewerage
- Storm
- Water Supply
- Street Light
- Landscape
- Earthworks
- Solid Waste

**City Level**
- Transition Zones
- Main Sewer
- Treatment Plant
- River Front

**Buildings**
- Community Halls
- Dispensaries

**Miscellaneous Activities**
- Surveys
- Evaluation
- MIS
- Monitoring

objective was not to find solutions unique to the slums but to explore the commonalties between the slums and the city and to integrate the two to make mutually beneficial interventions.

Slum networking set out five objectives: (1) a holistic approach to environmental issues in order to upgrade the slums and the entire city; (2) a significant reduction in the cost of utilities and housing; (3) the mobilization of material resources for the development of settlements; (4) the increase in community responsibility and control; and (5) the improvement of the overall quality of life in terms of education, health and income. The objectives were realized through innovative and low-cost engineering solutions. The designer gave priority to lowering and then paving the slum streets, so that they drain off excess rainwater during the monsoons; to placing a gully trap in each house for the removal of waste water and sewage; to installing a manhole-covered inspection pit for every six to eight houses; and to

The success of the Indore Habitat Project relies on three main components: physical works, community development and various monitoring and information gathering activities that support those programmes.

OPPOSITE and RIGHT Underground sewerage systems and an improved water supply system have been put in place in the slum colonies. The slum dwellers pay for and build their own toilets and connections to the water and sewerage systems. The investment enhances their quality of life and hence their pride in home ownership.

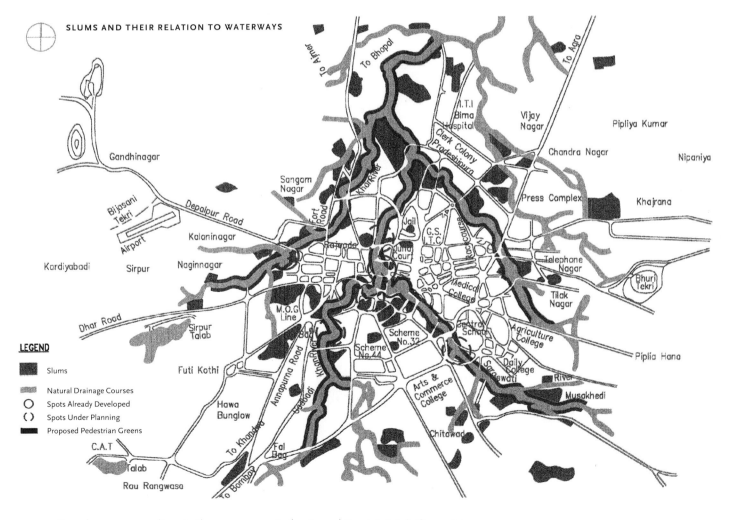

SLUMS AND THEIR RELATION TO WATERWAYS

LEGEND

- ■ Slums
- ▨ Natural Drainage Courses
- O Spots Already Developed
- ( ) Spots Under Planning
- ▬ Proposed Pedestrian Greens

connecting slum sewerage lines to the main artery along the river.

The solution was implemented at two levels. At the city level, a main sewerage artery funded by the Indore Development Authority and Great Britain's Overseas Development Administration (now the Department for International Development) was constructed along the riverbank at a cost of US $18,000,000. At

Once the piped sewerage system was in place it was possible to clean the rivers and restore historic riverside structures. This improvement to the slums had a citywide effect, reinvigorating urban life at the centre of Indore.

RIGHT To increase water levels at the *jheel*, where the Khan and Saraswati rivers meet, the banks of the river were lowered. This also accommodated terraced pathways that improve access to the main bridge.

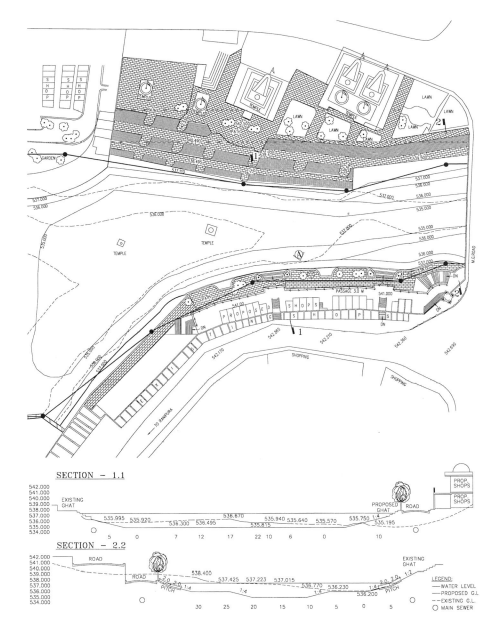

Indore. Once full of sewage and garbage, the *jheel* has been transformed into a waterfront area that has revitalized Indore's cultural heritage and the city as a whole. On one bank, two kilometres of riverfront have been landscaped with curved, paved walkways, flowering plants and shade trees. On the opposite bank, a two-level shopping arcade has been developed.

In the 1980s, slum improvement projects typically provided facilities such as community toilets and washrooms. Sharing such facilities gave rise to communal riots, crime and abuse. For privacy, women frequented the toilets early in the morning, where they were often subject to rape or assault. Now, with each house equipped with an individual toilet and washroom, not only is the housing upgraded, the slums are also nearly crime-free.

Alleviating poverty is a priority in developing countries but it consumes an enormous portion of national fiscal allocations and sustainability is often difficult, resulting in sporadic,

# Lepers Hospital Chopda Taluka, India

Architects: Per Christian Brynildsen

Completed 1985

nd Jan Olav Jensen

Client: Norwegian Free Evangelical Mission, India Trust

For the initiative of young architects in planning and building an institution for which society had made no provision. Using only the very limited available resources – techniques, labour and materials – they created a 'paradise garden', an attractive and friendly sheltering enclave, within a barren and hostile environment. Out of minimal architectural form, they devised a design of stark simplicity that radiates calm.

In the dry season, the Lepers Hospital is set in the middle of a rugged, desert-like terrain.

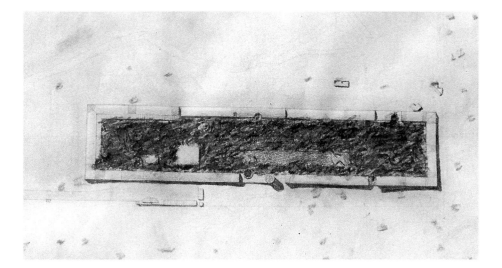

Leprosy, or Hansen's disease, affects about 3 per cent of the population in South Asia. Though now treatable with antibiotics, the illness is still wrought with superstition and fear. When the signs of leprosy can no longer be hidden, the afflicted are often expelled from their families, and among tribal peoples some lepers are even killed. Begging is the only way for thousands of these outcasts to survive, walking the roads between the villages and towns of the Indian subcontinent.

The Lepers Hospital, a refuge on the border of the hilly, forested Satpura preserve overlooking the cultivated plain of the Tapti River, is the first treatment centre for leprosy in the region. The project was initiated by Clara Lerberg, who, after fifty years as a missionary with the Norwegian Free Evangelical Mission in India, wanted to provide care for the indigent lepers who would appear, dressed in rags and begging, at her door. To support the project, local authorities donated a site outside Lasur village, about

13 kilometres from Chopda in the Jalgaon District of Maharashtra. When two young Norwegian architecture students came to visit in March 1983, Mrs Lerberg and her husband, Leif, asked them to draw a site plan, the first step in realizing their ambition to build a hospital.

In the midst of a study trip to India and Nepal, Jan Olav Jensen, himself the son of former missionaries in India, and Per Christian Brynildsen sketched a site plan for the Lerbergs, and then agreed to return for as long as needed to design the hospital and supervise its construction. While in Kathmandu they drew preliminary plans and sent them on to Chopda and Lasur for approvals. Three weeks after they returned to Chopda in June 1983, construction began with the digging of the hospital's foundations.

Maharashtra is known in India as the land of caves, forts and temples, but the Jalgaon District is quite remote from these landmarks. The rainy season lasts four months and often causes flooding; the

**ABOVE** The architects' conceptual sketch depicts a sanctuary that contains a 'paradise garden' in an otherwise bleak setting.

**OPPOSITE** In the rainy season the landscape of Chopda Taluka becomes rich and green, but wildlife and the constant threat of thievery are elements that the Lepers Hospital must protect against.

rest of the year is hot and dry and the landscape takes on a desert appearance. Tigers, leopards and other wild animals haunt the terrain at the edge of the jungle, and frequent highwaymen make the area even more dangerous. For safety reasons, most buildings are clustered in villages that are located near water and trees. The villagers harvest trees in the forest to be sold in nearby towns and breed animals for their milk or to sell at regularly held livestock auctions.

**ABOVE** The simple, linear buildings, only 4 metres wide, are made with load-bearing walls topped with shallow barrel vaults. The gently curved roof is sealed with broken glazed tile obtained from a nearby factory.

**OPPOSITE TOP** Section looking towards the doctor's quarters.

**OPPOSITE** From within the courtyard, the stone buildings – constructed entirely with local materials and by local workmen – provide a sense of protection and security for the patients and hospital staff.

the site. The roofs of the shallow brick
vaults were clad with broken glazed tiles
acquired from a nearby factory. White tiles
that reflect the sun's heat were laid over
the enclosed spaces, coloured tiles over
the open verandas. Jensen and Brynildsen
stayed thirteen months in Chopda,
overseeing as many as seventy workers
whose only machine tools were a truck
used to transport materials and a concrete
vibrator, used in the late stages of
construction. When the architects left to
return to school in September 1984, the
workers, by then experienced, continued
to build, and in July 1985 the first patients
and a nurse arrived to take up residence
in the hospital. At that point, the entire
project had cost only US $140,000.

A small, circular prayer space in the
courtyard encloses a shade-giving tree.
The interior is clad in blue and white
broken tiles sorted from the many colours
used on the hospital roof.

LEFT and BELOW The nurse's apartment and doctor's kitchen are two of the private spaces in the complex. A communal kitchen provides a hearth for cooking fires. Low windows admit daylight while reducing heat gain.

RIGHT In the guest apartment, as in all of the hospital's interior spaces, tie rods that hold the red stone walls in place are visible just below the vaulted brick ceiling.

Today the Lepers Hospital serves hundreds of outpatients. The thirty to forty patients who live in not only receive treatment but also work in the grain fields just outside the enclave and tend the buffaloes kept for their milk. In the courtyard, trees and flowers provide shade and beauty and the calm of the 'paradise garden'. For the lepers, the hospital is 'the door of hope' in a society that had previously made no provision for them.

**LEFT** and **BELOW** The men's ward can accommodate 32 patients. The end walls are perforated to facilitate air circulation. Each ward opens on to a covered veranda.

**RIGHT** The dining hall veranda and triangular porch off the women's 18-bed ward provide vistas of the planted courtyard, or paradise garden, and shaded places for outdoor relaxation.

LEFT and ABOVE Unique details in the modest, low-budget building are found in the window treatments. A stepped window in the guest bathroom, seen here from within and without, admits light from floor to ceiling.

OPPOSITE Various window types add visual interest to the long façades and often indicate the nature of the spaces inside. Clockwise: a window in the nurse's apartment; a pair of windows in the storage room; a floor-to-ceiling opening overlooking the guest apartment veranda.

# Salinger Residence Selangor, Malaysia

Architect: Jimmy C. S. Lim

Completed 1992

Standing high up on stilts, the wooden Salinger

Master Carpenter: **Ibrahim bin Adam**

Client: **Rudin and Munira Salinger**

For evolving a distinctive modern interpretation of the traditional

Malay wooden house raised on stilts, a structure with significant

ecological advantages and a welcome re-emphasis on timber in place

of now standardized building materials. The house superimposes

triangular spaces for indoor and outdoor living and enacts a symbolic

union between the modern and the traditional. It demonstrates that

high technology and energy-depleting services can be renounced if

sufficient craft and creativity are deployed, and that the deeper

meaning of a vernacular architectural tradition can be combined

with the surroundings of contemporary everyday life.

Built on a former rubber plantation 15 kilometres south of Kuala Lumpur, the Salinger Residence is a single-family house made exclusively of timber in the traditional ways of the Malays. Commissioned by Professor Rudin Salinger, who teaches physics at the nearby National University, and his wife, Munira Salinger, the house is a contemporary interpretation of traditional Malay wooden houses in which architect Jimmy C. S. Lim incorporated environmentally sensitive methods for building in the tropics.

The traditional Malay house is a post-and-beam hardwood structure raised on stilts and with infill panels of timber or bamboo. Its simple rectangular form, oriented towards Mecca, is topped with a large, overhanging pitched roof that maximizes natural ventilation systems and protects the house from monsoon rains and strong sunlight. A veranda, called the *anjung*, surrounds the house on three sides and is the social space for the family and visitors. This type of house is still found in the rural areas of Malaysia. Contemporary residential architecture in Malaysia, particularly around Kuala Lumpur, tends to be in high-rise apartment buildings or in row house developments in new towns. The garden villa, common in high-income areas, is usually constructed with concrete frame and brick infill. The villas appear in a variety of forms and sizes, but are generally finished with plaster and paint, and rely on energy-consuming air-conditioning systems for cooling.

Professor and Mrs Salinger specifically wanted a modern house that reflected their keen interest in Malay culture and their Islamic faith. They approached Lim with simple and specific requirements: two bedrooms, an open kitchen in which Professor Salinger could entertain while cooking and living spaces. Lim organized this basically tripartite programme in an open plan that places two equilateral triangles against one another: a large triangle to accommodate indoor living and a second, smaller triangle for outdoor

ABOVE Architect Jimmy C. S. Lim proposed a form made with superimposed triangles in this preliminary design sketch.

OPPOSITE The long façades and acute angles created by the triangular plan give the house a variety of appearances, including a ship-like prow, behind which is the guest bedroom.

SALINGER RESIDENCE

85

living. The interior space flows naturally to the outdoors, and the open plan ensures natural cross-ventilation.

One of the driving forces in Lim's work is his concern for sustainable ecological principles with minimal environmental impact. He placed the Salingers' house at a high point on their three-acre wooded lot in order to reduce water run-off during the monsoon rains, and oriented it to capture the prevailing breezes. Lifting the house up on stilts in the style of traditional Malay houses, Lim also reduced the impact of the building on the land, eliminated the need for major excavation work and retained the natural sloping contours of the site.

Many elements indigenous to Malay architecture were incorporated in the design, including the use of local hardwood, called *chengal*, and elaborate roof forms with large overhangs. Variation and interpretation occur in Lim's triangular plan, which creates a unique

ABOVE and OPPOSITE The house sits at one side of its three-acre site, which allows for a long approach through the treed lot. The timber columns surround a stone core that contains the entrance to the elevated, two-storey house. In the shaded outdoor area beneath the main living floor the Salingers conduct classes in batik. The external timber is left in its natural state, treated only with *minyak daman*, the oil from the *daman* tree, which improves the wood's water resistance.

87

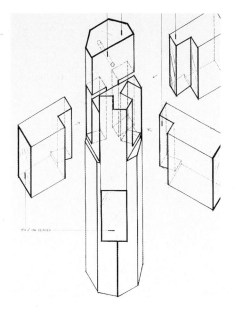

**TOP** The house was built in the traditional Malay post-and-beam timber style by a team of carpenters. With the help of the master carpenter, the architect designed the house to be made solely by using wooden dowels and joints as fasteners.

**ABOVE** East–west section facing south. The house is oriented to take advantage of the prevailing breezes for natural cooling.

**LEFT** The staircase and stone core were the first elements to be built. Then the structural columns independent of the stairs were put into place with a series of pulleys, hoists and ramps. As the stone structure was built up, the timber structure was tied into it.

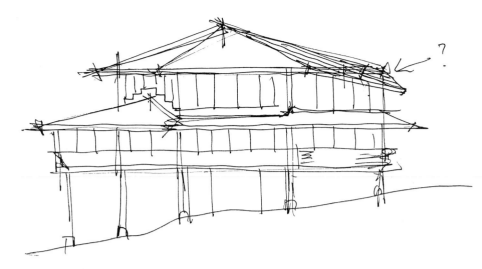

geometric form, yet one in which one wall still faces Mecca, as in traditional Malay houses. The smaller, outdoor triangle appears to be simply a veranda extension of the living room, but it also supports a *wakaf*, or roof, for an outdoor, covered prayer space like the ones traditionally provided for field workers. Circulation in the two-storey structure is through a granite-clad central core that anchors the house to the ground and tapers as it rises.

Professor Salinger hired a team of traditional Malay carpenters from Kelantan, on the east coast of Malaysia,

ABOVE Conceptual sketch.

BELOW The roof was assembled on the ground and then taken apart. The pieces were lifted by a series of ropes and pulleys and then reassembled 16 metres above ground in mid-air. The roof tiles were affixed before the floors below were built in order to shield the construction from the weather.

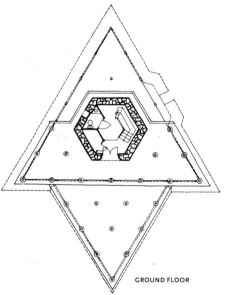

GROUND FLOOR

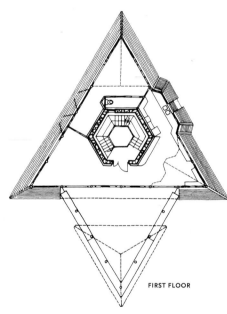

FIRST FLOOR

SECOND FLOOR

**ABOVE** The open triangular plan surrounds a central core that tapers as it rises from grade to the second storey. Living spaces and a guest room are on the first floor and the master bedroom on the second.

**OPPOSITE** Ventilation grilles over the windows and at high points in the roof aid in the natural cooling of the house. A ceiling fan over the living room is the only electrified cooling element.

to build the house, and Lim designed the joinery details accordingly. Master carpenter Ibrahim bin Adam especially selected three *chengal* trees, noted for their resistance to water and termites, to be used for the house. These were cut from two different forests and hauled in sections to the site. The team of six carpenters, working three or four at a time, took six and a half years to cut each wooden joint and assemble the house. No

metal fasteners were used except for the few nails needed to secure the floor of the *anjung*. The only machinery used was a small cement mixer. The timbers themselves were erected through a system of ropes and pulleys.

The Salinger Residence is unique in its time and place, and now, because of the Salingers' interests, is not only a private home but a centre for traditional practices such as Malay cooking and batik. While

ABOVE and BELOW  The triangular veranda, or *anjung*, off the living room is partially shaded by a *wakaf*. The *wakaf* is a gift of money that is manifested as a structure built to provide a shaded prayer space for men working in the rice fields. The floor boards of the *anjung*, set in a triangular pattern, are the only pieces in the house that are attached with nails.

traditional in its material and its method of construction, the house is a modern building, not simply because it is equipped with modern conveniences but because Lim interprets rather than imitates Malay tradition. The sharp

angles of the triangular forms that thrust outwards above the site simultaneously recall Malay structures and announce that this work of architecture is something completely contemporary.

RIGHT and BELOW The house fans out from a stone core. Cross-ventilation is enhanced by the openness of the veranda floor, which also serves to shade work areas adjacent to the core.

OPPOSITE TOP and ABOVE The public
spaces – cooking, dining and living – are
all on the first floor. The ventilation grilles
over the windows are made up of three
vertical pieces of wood crossed by three
horizontal pieces, known locally as *sekawan
tiga*, or three friends. The grilles are the
only decorative feature on the façade.

OPPOSITE The open living room space
moves naturally out to the veranda, a
social gathering place in traditional
Malay houses.

RIGHT The staircase leads to the top
floor where the main bedroom is located.

# Tuwaiq Palace Riyadh, Saudi Arabia

Architects: OHO Joint Venture: Atelier

Completed 1985

Tuwaiq Palace stands on a high limestone
plateau that overlooks the palm-filled Wadi
Hanifa at the edge of Riyadh.

# Frei Otto; Büro Happold and Omrania

## Client: Arriyadh Development Authority

For its architectural qualities and its setting within a dramatic landscape, the idea of a soft fortification, its hard and soft spaces, its combination of concrete, stone, tensile structures and landscaping. Although accessible to a limited public, its spatial organization and the differentiation between indoor and outdoor spaces works very well. One of its many merits is that the design relies on the interpretation of local formalism and relates it to a contemporary architectural language. In not trying to camouflage its volume by 'crumbling' its form, the building has an inherent strength.

Tuwaiq Palace is the central cultural facility for the diplomatic quarter in Riyadh, an impressive area of foreign diplomatic missions developed on the northwest side of the city in the early 1980s. The building stands on a high limestone plateau that juts toward the palm-filled Wadi Hanifa and the expansive desert beyond, areas that form part of a natural desert reserve. The hot and arid climate of central Arabia and its violent sandstorms have had a distinct effect on the style of building in Riyadh. This history includes old fortresses – an old watchtower still stands at one edge of the plateau, from which the routes to old Riyadh were once guarded – and tents, which were usually black and made of wool. The vernacular architecture of the region, called Najdi, includes mud walls and battered, curving towers with protected courtyards and apertures just large enough to admit daylight and air currents.

When a limited design competition for Tuwaiq Palace was organized in Spring 1980, the environment and architectural heritage of central Arabia were key criteria, but a clear mandate also stated: 'Any form of revival style or copying traditional patterns and details in old or new material, thus creating false 'neo-Orientalism', will not be acceptable.' In other words, no obvious imitations of traditional architecture would be considered. The competition responses of Frei Otto of Germany and Omrania of Riyadh each attracted attention – Otto's for the use of tents and Omrania's for a terraced building that engaged the landscape. The overseeing Arriyadh Development Authority, guided primarily by Dr Muhammad bin Abdul-Aziz Al-Shaikh, asked the two firms to work together. The first task of the not always easy marriage was to make a detailed programming report with the help of the British engineering firm Büro Happold.

A number of different design concepts were tried. Omrania worked out a terraced building with a courtyard. Otto worked

ABOVE The cultural and social facility is in the heart of the new diplomatic quarter of Riyadh, which today is composed of more than forty embassies, all built since the foreign diplomatic missions were moved from Jeddah beginning in 1983.

OPPOSITE The sinuous, terraced walls of the building provide numerous vistas of the desert beyond and the manmade oasis contained at the centre of the winding form.

TUWAIQ PALACE

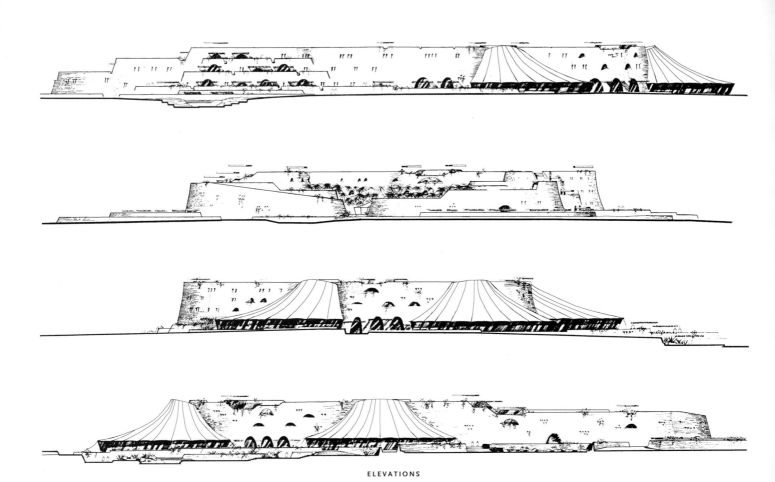

ELEVATIONS

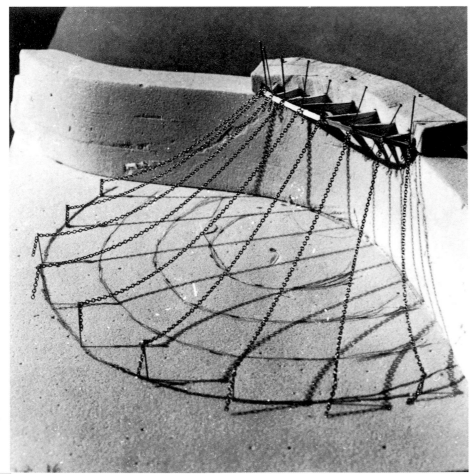

with irregular 'fingers' extruding from a core. When these were blended they made an irregular form that combined platforms, 'caves', or carved-out spaces and sinuous perimeter walls. This led to the notion of treating the whole building as a snaking, 800-metre-long wall that wrapped around and protected a green garden, or oasis. Large programmes such as the restaurant and swimming pool would be accommodated in giant tent structures fanning out from the wall. Thus the design began to touch on two local archetypes, the fortress and the tent, as well as incorporate the 'natural' phenomenon of the oasis. In their combination, these elements suggested a new building typology with a special relationship to its region.

OPPOSITE and RIGHT After a design
competition, the finalists were asked to
work together to create a joint scheme. After
extensive study, the tent structures of Frei
Otto and Büro Happold were eventually
married with the sinuous wall building
proposed by Omrania.

1  Reception
2  Lounge
3  Restaurant
4  Banquet hall
5  Guest accommodation
6  Multi-purpose hall
7  Children's swimming pool
8  Main swimming pool

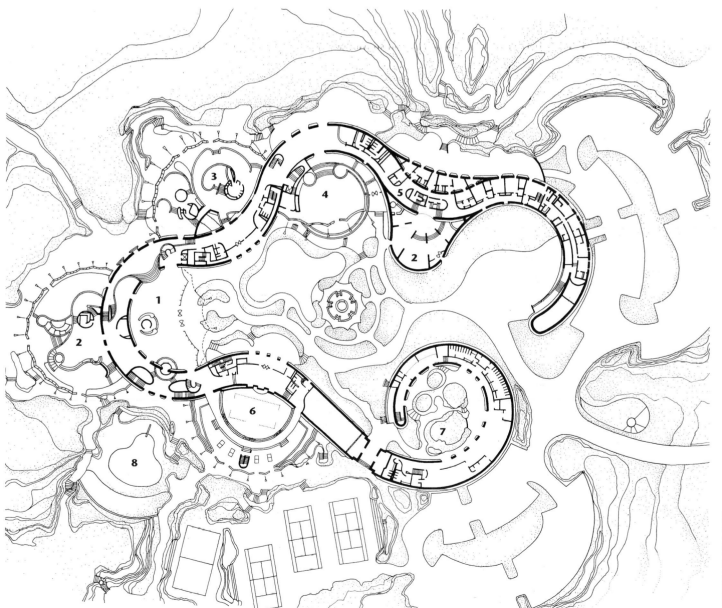

BELOW and RIGHT Tuwaiq Palace is
approached primarily by car. The main
entrance is from within the courtyard.
The reinforced concrete walls, which
lean back slightly, are clad in Riyadh
limestone block that is compatible with
the desert colours. Visitors can stroll along
the rooftop to enjoy views of the desert.

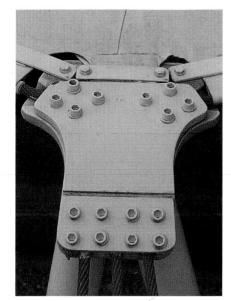

**ABOVE** and **LEFT** The white Teflon-coated tents are supported by cables that are attached radially to the wall by fan-shaped steel masts. The tents are enclosed with glass walls that overlook the desert and the various outdoor sports facilities. At ground level the tent cables are supported by inclined hinged masts and tied to anchor blocks.

The blue tents that face the inner gardens are directly attached to the wall without support masts and are punctuated with fan-shaped skylights that cast sun and shadow on the interior walls. Outdoor sport facilities adjacent to the building complement the indoor sport facilities under the tents.

BELOW and OPPOSITE Landscaping around the building echoes the rocky desert surroundings with plantings and rock walls.

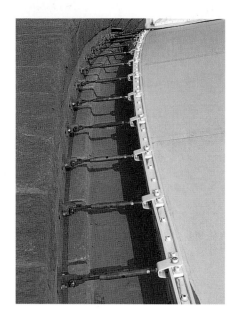

ABOVE and LEFT  At one end of Tuwaiq Palace the sinuous wall wraps around and protects outdoor swimming pools. The introduction of landscaping and rock formations integrate the pool area with other site conditions, including the central garden and the rocky plateau on which the building stands. In the background, a blue tent protects a courtyard entrance to the facility.

From a distance, Tuwaiq Palace appears to be a ruined fort surrounded by an encampment. The white tents are almost luminous and effectively contrast with the stone walls. In working with such complex geometries, the designers ran the risk of awkward joints between many elements and failed to work out an entirely consistent grammar of detail for the building. Nonetheless, intriguing grottoes and walkways provide ever-changing vistas and moods, in a balanced combination of formality and fun.

Much Saudi development in the 1980s consisted of a slavish and glossy imitation of Western building models. Tuwaiq Palace is a bold departure from this trend, touching instead upon easily understood signals from past desert civilizations: tents, walls, oases, fortifications and so forth. This reinterpretation is a daring confrontation with and successful marriage of tradition and high tech.

TUWAIQ PALACE

# Alhamra Arts Council Lahore, Pakistan

Architect: Nayyar Ali Dada

Completed 1992

The Alhamra Arts Council buildings
constitute a performing and visual arts
complex that has become Pakistan's
leading cultural centre.

For having created a significant cultural complex as a continuously used art forum in the city of Lahore, while interpreting traditional Mughal style by way of a modern architectural vocabulary. The whole complex is a rare example of flexible spaces, and has enabled several additions to be made over time, each of which has in turn enhanced, rather than detracted from, its overall architectural value. This is a very popular and successful public building, projecting its complexities in a simple and powerful manner.

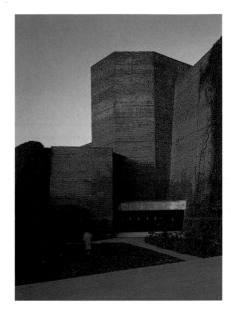

A former Imperial Mughal capital, Lahore is a city rich in an architectural heritage that reflects the political fortunes of its historic conquerors. The modern city was organized along a pattern set primarily by the British during their hundred-year colonial rule of the Indian subcontinent. The Alhamra Arts Council is located at a corner of the old Mall Road that was laid during the colonial period to connect the city centre with a military cantonment to the southeast. At one end of the Mall, now called Shahrah Quaid-e Azam after Pakistan's founding father, are large, brick, state buildings intermixed with structures reflecting nineteenth-century British Neo-Gothic and local Mughal traditions. The other end, further from the city centre, is less intensely developed and retains the characteristics of a grand boulevard.

When the British left the subcontinent in 1947, Pakistan emerged as a country in search of a cultural identity. In the immediate postcolonial period, two architectural directions developed, one based on the International Style and heavily influenced by Le Corbusier, the other on the Brutalist style of the 1960s. Attempts to replicate local motifs in modern building materials led to a hybrid mix of mannerist and eclectic effects.

Other arts were also developing during the immediate postcolonial period, including the Alhamra Arts Council, a small, new, nongovernmental group interested in theatre and art. The government of Pakistan gave the council its present site, which for years was occupied only by a small hut and some temporary structures. Most of the council's theatrical productions were held in the open air.

By the early 1970s, the council had a major cultural presence in Pakistan, and its members began consulting with architects to plan a permanent building. Nayyar Ali Dada, then a member of the council, was retained to design a complex to be built in four phases, the first of which would be a thousand-seat theatre. As the first phase was completed in 1979, ownership of the site was questioned.

OPPOSITE and ABOVE Nayyar Ali Dada developed a series of polygonal shapes that, with slightly tapered walls built in red brick, recall historic, red sandstone Mughal monuments in the city. The four-phase building programme included an art gallery (opposite) and three theatres.

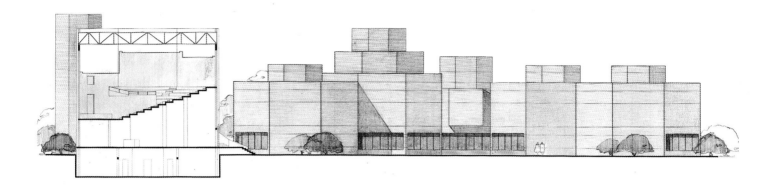

was the use of solid red-brick walls. A major departure from Dada's earlier work in concrete, the brick recalled the red sandstone of the Mughal Lahore Fort and Badshahi Mosque, the two most important historic buildings in the city. The locally produced brick was also the most economical material, a prime consideration given the small amount budgeted for the complex.

The first-phase theatre building, the only piece of the complex visible from the

THESE PAGES  The arrangement of the various facilities has led to the development of soft, public green spaces between them. The mostly windowless, massive walls, which are the result of the Arts Council's programmes, are articulated with brick coursing and sometimes alleviated by colourful murals and sculpture installations.

THESE PAGES A dramatic lobby
welcomes visitors to the largest theatre,
which is accessed by two large and
simply detailed stairs. The two-level lobby
is partially tucked under the theatre seating,
which can be seen in the stepped ceiling
plan. The simple, broad stairs that lead
to the theatre are in stark contrast with
the tight spiral staircase that links the
floors in the nearby two-storey art
gallery building.

THESE PAGES The art gallery, built in phase two, is composed of four symmetrically arranged octagons. The two central octagons are double-height exhibition spaces, which are connected by a mezzanine level. The only natural light source is through light shafts in the ceilings.

 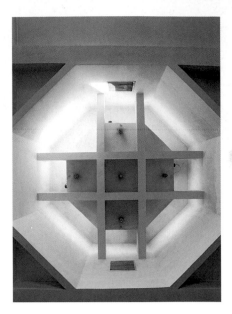

and traditional music performances, the other containing offices.

Since phase four was completed in 1992, more than three thousand people a day have used the Alhamra Arts Council complex. The courtyard and green spaces that flow between the various facilities are busy by midday. The theatres accommodate two sold-out performances each night. The galleries are used for exhibitions of artists' and students' work, and the practice rooms are regularly occupied by music students and their teachers.

Through the use of indigenous materials and traditional forms, Dada has innovatively recalled the images of the Mughal forts without the use of clichés or symbols. The Alhamra Arts Council is an important response to the issue of identity in a developing country. Together with its programme of theatre, music and art, the complex also restores Lahore's role as the cultural capital of Pakistan.

# Vidhan Bhavan Bhopal, India

Architect: **Charles Correa**

Completed 1996

Vidhan Bhavan sits on the crest of the Arera
Hill, overlooking the Madhya Pradesh capital
city of Bhopal.

For the numerous qualities of this ambitious project, its heroic scale and the creation of an ensemble that provides a wide range of spatial experiences as one moves through the complex. The dangers of creating spatial chaos in order to accommodate its multiple functions have been successfully avoided with a circular fortified enclosure. Despite the use of axial planning and the formal organization of spaces punctuated by mythical and historical symbols, the building uses the vocabulary of modern architecture and avoids the use of pastiche folk motifs, thereby contributing to the contemporary idiom of the architecture of Islamic societies. The use of colour and of murals painted by modern folk artists is innovative and adds a degree of lightness to the internal spaces, in the process reviving the historical practice of painting interiors in public buildings and making it part of a new modern idiom for the region.

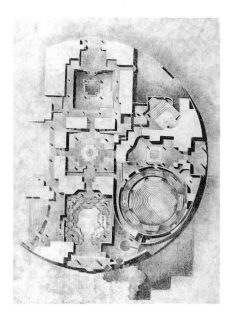

Vidhan Bhavan, the new State Assembly for the government of Madhya Pradesh, reflects architect Charles Correa's concern for humanist values in the seat of governmental authority. Rather than design a monument to political power, Correa organized the large government facility with a series of courtyards and pathways, which, while meeting the requirements of administrative and legislative functions, break down what could have been a monolithic whole into a series of urban spaces that welcome public participation.

Vidhan Bhavan sits on the crest of the Arera Hill, overlooking the capital city of Bhopal and its historic Muslim monuments. It replaces a colonial-era structure that had served as a guesthouse for the viceroy of India before becoming the State Assembly building after the Indian States Reorganisation Act of 1956. The approach to the hilltop site is via a winding road; hence the plan of the building was developed as a circle. This gave the 32,000-square-metre building a

unity and presence regardless of the direction from which it was approached. While the circular form recalls Correa's interest in the mandala, here it primarily reflects Indian cultural and historical references, including the Parliament Building in New Delhi and the ancient Buddhist stupa in nearby Sanchi.

The programme for the State Assembly specified four main functions: the Vidhan Sabha, or Lower House, for 366 members; the Vidhan Parishad, or Upper House, for seventy-five members; the Combined Hall; and the Library. It also required a host of other facilities: offices for state ministers and their staffs; committee meeting rooms; suites for the Speaker of the House; offices for the Chief Secretary of the Government and the Chief Minister; and areas for cafeterias and administrative staffs. These programmes also required various means of access for three kinds of users: the legislators, the VIPs and the general public, who, for security reasons, needed to have separate paths of circulation to the various halls.

OPPOSITE The public entrance to the State Assembly building is flanked by a fountain in the shape of Madhya Pradesh's boundaries. The fountain spills into a larger pool that reaches towards the VIP entrance to the building.

VIDHAN BHAVAN

131

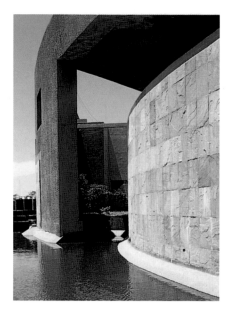

Access to the building is through three strikingly different entrances that punctuate the circle at 90-degree intervals: a door surrounded by grillework for the assembly members; a bold blue-and-white striped VIP entrance; and a public entrance that penetrates deep into the circle via the Court of the People. The entrances set up a clear cross-axis within. Circulation, however, is more labyrinthine, following the edges of the interior, open-air courtyards that Correa calls 'gardens

VIDHAN BHAVAN

135

ABOVE Correa cuts into the perfect circle to reveal the curved form of the Vidhan Parishad (Upper House) that clings to the wall of the tower form. To the left is the VIP entrance; the right, the entry for the legislators.

within gardens' and around which the many administrative offices are organized. After entering the Court of the People at the public entrance, for example, visitors pass through a checkpoint and then follow different routes to reach the various viewing galleries that overlook the three main

halls. Along the way they cross bridges and ramps, which, winding like the ritual circumambulatory *pradakshina* around the stupa, allow them to experience the principal spaces of the complex. Five central courtyards or halls occupy the cross-axial space, and the four outer 'corners' at the perimeter contain the specialized spaces of the legislative houses, the Combined Hall and the Library.

Although its commanding hilltop site and unusual colours and form attract the eye, the Vidhan Bhavan is conceived not as a monument but as a city within the city, both in its roofline profile and in plan. Correa's formal references to other Indian buildings – the dome of the Vidhan Sabha, a small tower and the open-air courtyards – are organized in the circular plan to create an urban atmosphere. The local red stone, handmade ceramic tiles and paint typically found in area buildings de-emphasize the idea of a governmental monument as well.

VIDHAN BHAVAN

The blue-and-white diagonal stripes herald the VIP entrance. Just inside, an elegant Legislators' Foyer provides access to the legislative chambers. Through the brilliantly coloured gate one enters the Vidhan Sabha; a set of doors opposite, surrounded by a giant wall mural, open into the Vidhan Parishad.

VIDHAN BHAVAN

RIGHT and BELOW The Central Hall
links the legislators' and VIP entrances.
An oculus in the ceiling opens the hall to
the sky and mirrors the mandala shape
embedded in the floor. Geometric forms
appear in the floors throughout the
building.

OPPOSITE In the library, a stairway
leads to a second level. Paintings on the
walls and throughout the building are
by contemporary artists living in
Madhya Pradesh.

Throughout the building there are
references to Madhya Pradesh itself.
The use of gateways, enclosures, courts,
small domes and other architectural
details develops a new imagery based
on local forms. A reflecting pool at the
public entrance is in the shape of the
state, and the walls of the Court of the
People are painted with the colourful
mythic images of the tribal people of
Bastar. Large contemporary murals,
sculpture and paintings by local artists
found throughout the building are
vivid examples of the breadth of
artistic traditions in the state. With this
integration of local art and architectural
traditions in a modern building, the
Vidhan Bhavan not only houses Madhya
Pradesh's governmental representatives,
it represents Madhya Pradesh itself.
At the same time, it breaks the myth
that modern architecture cannot be
adapted to Asian nations and
environments.

LEFT The Cabinet Room

BELOW The wavy form of the Combined Hall is replayed inside in the swooping ceiling and along the walls.

OPPOSITE The domed Vidhan Sabha seats 366 members. The public can observe the proceedings from upper viewing galleries.

# Master Jury Discussion

## Mohammed Arkoun

The Award has now existed for twenty years and has a history. This history is constraining in the sense that we have already illustrated, through the Award's previous cycles, many aspects of architecture. We were thinking in the spirit of the contexts prevailing during the 1980s and 1990s. Now we are obliged to think in another 'frame', which is the frame of globalization. In my view, the principal message that this jury – the last jury of this century – could send is to say that the Award should move away from the frame of decolonization, of the cold war, of under-development and overdevelopment, etc. Today is a totally different scene. We have to integrate the forces of globalization affecting all societies, whether Western or what we call the 'Third World', to create a frame for the next cycles of thinking. This will be difficult, given the projects we have, because these projects belong to the past, and I am describing the future. The principal point is not to give awards to projects that just repeat what has been already awarded and illustrated in previous Award cycles. This exercise is going to be difficult. We have to pay attention in order to introduce new aspects through the projects that will be awarded. This can give us the possibility of common criteria for our evaluation of the projects.

## Fredric Jameson

I agree that it is very important for us to see this as a projection of problems rather than as solutions on which we don't necessarily all agree. In that spirit, I would like to foreground these problems a little more sharply. Perhaps something like 'urbanism and architectural aesthetics under globalization' defines the direction that we're trying to grapple with a little more clearly. Because I think the problem of urbanism must come out. Globalization is becoming a very frequently used word, but it still very pointedly brings out the dilemmas.

## Romi Khosla

I have some difficulties with trying to portray the Award as a pluralistic repetition. To me, the last six cycles of the Award represent and question the responsibilities of architects as globalization increases. The modern architect has probably lost the social content that was the essence of modern architecture. In the last ten or fifteen years, the social agenda has disappeared, big money has moved to modern architecture and the essence of the modern message has been lost. To me, the Award is still saying that this is not the way for architecture to go. Architecture has a very important role to play in terms of the thinking and the discussions about why change occurs in society. A modern architect cannot simply get a major building financed and with it portray the glory of modern architecture, because the spirit of modernism is missing, perhaps due to the collapse of social responsibility. I feel that the Award is still saying that this is the responsibility of architecture, even in conservation projects. The rehabilitation in Hebron, for example, is about community social housing. If we are looking for a global message to tell to the architectural profession about wider responsibility, this is a great eye-opener to me. You cannot simply confine yourself to building. At the edge of Europe, huge areas of nations are in the reformulation process, and the role of architecture is very critical precisely because these societies are being reformed. I think we are talking about architecture that has a different role to play than from what we see in the media. We are realigning the perceptions of architecture with social responsibility. The projects that we see in the history of the Award are essentially about catching a huge territory within architecture. Today, for example, conservation has by and large disappeared as an architectural activity; it is confined to experts who are concerned with the technicalities of conservation. In the Award, this conservation movement has become part of a community; it is not just one building restored out of context. When we look at a slum operation, when we look at a housing project, we ask, what is the role of the community?

### Mohammed Arkoun

Are there shared values in the new trends of architecture? In the concept of globalization? We must use a question mark if we are not bringing values that we know and would want to promote. There is the Muslim world and the rest of the world, and there is the West and the rest of the world. We are all bothered by the problem of values and their use. The Muslim world is still looking to Islam as something that warrants the permanence of values that are outside of any criticism. We have to pay attention to this. I am not totally opposing globalization: on the contrary. But we have to think about the Islamic discourse, which is strongly, even violently, opposed to the forces of globalization as it is imposed by the West. The Islamic discourse claims that it has values which are almost eternal and are opposed to the pressures exercised by globalization. Approaching this Muslim claim of eternal values with the critical values of reflection, we can make a kind of transition, maintaining the criticism of Islamic discourse not only in architecture, but in all aspects of life.

Shared values means that we are thinking about urbanism and architecture in the world, not simply for Muslims, and that we are acting within the process and constraints of globalization. For me, this is extremely important, because it maintains the option for the Award to have a critical approach to what is going on, not only in the Muslim world but also in the world that includes the West. We're thinking about architecture and urbanism that affect the entire world by focusing on a part of the world that has special pressures especially related to religion. When we say 'religion', we say 'values'; thus the problem for us is to criticize these values, not only in the field of architecture but also in other fields. The concern for urbanism and architecture opens new horizons to enrich our thinking. Our exercise will make sense for the problems of architecture and will make sense for the future of the Award. If we don't integrate this, the Award will become totally ritualized, repeating what has already been done successfully simply because it was a new approach to problems of architecture in the Islamic world. If we continue giving almost the same message, the Award will be totally ritualized and will not be seen as an innovative effort to contribute to architecture and urbanism and their changing problems.

### Romi Khosla

I would still like to see a narrower context, one concerned with the responsibilities of architecture under globalization. This also emphasizes the changing role of the architect.

### Arif Hasan

It is important to reflect on what globalization means to the built environment. In the cities I know, several important things have happened. One is the rise of a powerful corporate sector, which is still unsure of itself. The second is the marginalization of large sections of the population that are becoming increasingly poor and, in the process, becoming politicized, a trend that is likely to increase. This marginalized population is very different from the marginalized populations of twenty years ago; it is young, urban and no longer a migrant population. In the next twenty years, the migrant population will be minuscule, for people will have been born in and grown up in the cities, and will have a claim on the cities. They will not be 'pioneers' who have come to look for a better livelihood; they will be city people with city values. This is a very important cultural change that is taking place. In my city, Karachi, that change is already producing enormous problems, and the structural adjustment, which is an important part of the globalization process, is increasing the problem further. Another aspect is the weakening of government agencies, for two reasons: first, the cutback in government funds is being replaced by privatization, and, second, the role of international contractors and consultants is increasing in these works, whether in the Far East, South Asia or wherever. In the physical sense these are not new problems, but the social, cultural and stateless aspects of these problems are all new. In the poorer countries, you have the makings of an enormous conflict, not only a political conflict, but a conflict of values, and how the victims of this change are going to articulate themselves. This is important. What will their manner of articulation be? The political, the cultural, the built environment and the delivery of social services have actually become inseparable things. They are very much of a whole, and it is becoming increasingly difficult to slice them into pieces. Indonesia tried to slice them – so did Thailand and Korea – and it has not worked.

The projects we are considering here suggest important changes from similar projects in the past; they are responding to new realities. Hebron Old Town represents a new reality that is asserting itself in political terms – the conservation aspects are not all that important. Similarly, in Indore there is a whole new way of looking at the environment of the city. It is not an old kampung improvement project or an area-upgrading project; new trends do emerge. They may not be articulated as such but they are there, and they reflect the realities that I just mentioned. Another factor due to globalization is the rise of economies in the services sector, through which the middle class has grown substantially. Contractors are building a jungle of what I call the 'new vernacular' of apartment blocks to meet middle-class housing needs. This is a very important aspect of the city today, because it is shaping the visible environment more than anything else. In most cases, this is not the work of an architect. Architects sign the plans, but almost everywhere, it is the work of contractors. Take Jakarta, Bangkok, Bombay, Karachi, Lahore; the shape of the city and its land-use patterns have changed because of this kind of intervention. This has to do with values, this whole new world, and its repercussions.

### Mohammed Arkoun

Values seen in a secular manner.

### Arif Hasan

In a rational, secular manner.

### Fredric Jameson

What role or significance would you place on the question of regionalism in your description? Is there a new regionalism that intervenes in this, either as a problem or as a solution, or do you think global organization is such that we need not stress that aspect of it?

### Arif Hasan

I think regionalism – and I may be wrong – is a dying force. You can express a certain detail of form and establish some continuity, but if you look at culture today, especially in our context, there are two major trends. There is an assimilation that is very powerful and very forceful in music and literature, in all media, and, simultaneously, an emphasis on ethnicity and small groupings. There is also a very strong emphasis on clan, which had disappeared and now is reasserting itself in the Far East and Central Asia, especially after so many years of Soviet rule. But that is not regionalism. I think that is identity not of a nation as such, but a smaller identity based on a language.

### Mohammed Arkoun

The problem of regionalism is very important and is a very good example to illustrate the differences between what is going on in the rest of the world and what is going on in the 'commanding' world, if I may say. Regionalization in Europe today is taking a very important course. The political mode in Europe is towards the European Union, which is a larger political space, one that has reduced and controlled cultural expressions of regionalism to build one nation with one national culture. Because of the pressure on a country like France, which is the most centralizing nation-state since the French Revolution, we see, for the first time in the history of France, trends towards a redefinition of regions, *les provinces françaises*, which had been totally put down by the nation-state. On the contrary, look at what is happening in the Muslim world for this problem. Islam, used as a universalizing ideology, is pushing down any regional cultural expression. I see it in my own country of Algeria. We have a Berber architecture that is totally different from what we call 'Islamic' architecture. This is an example of how we have to bring elements of comparison to the Award that make people reflect about the search for an Islamic identity. The Technical Reviewers almost all integrated the idea that the Award is illustrating an Islamic identity. This means that we have not delivered a very clear message for almost twenty years. We are not free from this image. Through the problem of regionalism, we can bring this issue back again.

### Dogan Tekeli

There seem to be two main directions in our thinking. One is urbanism, architecture and globalization, which are more universal; the other one is about values – shared values – which has a more specific meaning. Can we combine the two somehow? Can we find something in between and emphasize the values? Because values are important; without them, urbanism, architecture and globalization become sterile.

### Mohammed Arkoun

One of the responses of societies to the pressures of globalization is to affirm their own values. This is seen in the context of pluralism, which is another current word, and there is a clash of cultures and civilizations. Are there *shared* values? Because there are *conflicting* values. The problem is to investigate, and for the Award to reflect on, the present clash between values, and the ways to share values. The West is imposing, all over the world, what we call 'globalization', and the very weak societies are trying to defend themselves because they feel that what they call 'values' are being threatened. But, rather than focus on the clash as violence, we are trying to find peaceful answers through a search of the concrete terrain of architecture and urbanism. This is the genius of the Award: to approach the problems of cultures and of societies through architecture and urbanism.

### Arif Hasan

In our discussions, the aspect of values is paramount. We should look at these projects through the aspect of values.

### Yuswadi Saliya

If we give a prize to a work of architecture that is similar to one that was awarded fifteen years ago, we don't seem to be advancing anything. Is it proper for us to keep giving prizes to very similar kinds of architecture?

### Arata Isozaki

I came here as an architect, so I am looking at all the entries from an architectural point of view. I didn't find any interesting architectural design. If I follow a so-called modernist or post-modernist view, I have trouble with how to establish my own evaluation at this table. Probably we won't find modern architecture, or post-modern architecture, or so-called 'outside of the Islamic world' architecture. We won't find any definite trends because very little Islamic architecture is in the same position as modern or post-modern architecture. If we try to evaluate projects from every side, from the modern architecture side or the Islamic architecture side, there are no definite conclusions, no common fields. So, I am trying to find a different point of view, probably a more geopolitical view of architecture, which probably represents two different cultures, or two different waves of architecture – for example, modern and Islamic architecture, or newly developed technology versus historical architecture. We have many projects where two, three or four different forces are coming together, and through this conflict we have to find architectural solutions; not seek the 'pure' idea of modern architecture or 'pure' Islamic architecture, but something more interesting, perhaps something conflicting. I would like to find out whether there are some interesting architectural solutions based on this conflict. For me, that is the most interesting subject. In looking for conflict, the most interesting things are not in the centre of the Islamic world, but are more on the fringe, where local traditions are conflicting with new technology and developing new ideas, new solutions.

### Mohammed Arkoun

There is something very important in what Isozaki says. He used the words 'modern' and 'technology', and we are facing an architecture still wanting to retain traditions. He also said that this traditional architecture could not be an alternative against the power of new technologies and against the references that we make almost mechanically to what we call 'modern'. This is a major point for our process of thinking, because in Muslim societies we have exactly these three forces operating; in all the projects, we have a reference to something we call 'modern', but European 'modernity', in its classical expression, has never been assimilated in the Islamic world, not in the domain of thinking, in philosophy, in theology, in history as a discipline, or in the domain of architecture. Since the nineteenth century, there has been resistance to what Europe calls 'modernity', 'resistance' because of the necessity of liberation from colonialism, the 'resistance' to imperialism, and now the 'resistance' of the big Islamic model against Westernization in general. These societies resisted modernity and thus did not fully integrate the positive aspects of modernity. This resistance continues and is translated through the need to restore, to conserve, etc. And now come the powerful technologies and new markets, even stronger than they were in the 1960s, '70s and '80s. Resistance is now almost impossible because of these powerful markets and technologies. So we have to ask, 'What are we awarding'? Are we awarding projects which illustrate what I would call a 'wrong resistance'? 'Wrong' because it is based on ideological resistance, not on something that has been in Islamic thought, starting from theology? There has been no single innovative position in theology in the Islamic world since the nineteenth century. Regardless of geography, we have to think of this resistance and the true arguments that legitimize this resistance.

### Romi Khosla

How we define architecture, and the whole of architecture itself, are split between the modern tradition and countries where the modern tradition did not take root. These latter are metaphors of resistance to modernism, no doubt. Modernism is surely regarded as something more detached and isolated. Industry now enables you to have any form you like, so even form has become arbitrary. Somewhere along the line, the role and the social context of the architect were also isolated. In these societies, where there are metaphors of resistance, the role of the architect is being considered differently. There is value in looking not only at the form, but at the activity and the relationships between the professionals and communities that have produced these metaphors of resistance.

### Dogan Tekeli

Those are theoretical considerations. Mr Isozaki made a practical proposal to consider the theoretical basis of what is going on at the periphery of the Islamic world. Professor Arkoun describes it as a resistance to modernism.

### Fredric Jameson

It seems to me that you are calling for new categories. The category 'metaphors of resistance' would be a very interesting one to retain for future discussions.

### Romi Khosla

Arata, I still don't understand what you mean by 'the periphery'.

### Arata Isozaki

There are two meanings: first, the topographical fringe, which is like an edge of the Islamic world, and, second, a social class, a lower-class condition: I have both of these ideas in my thinking.

**Romi Khosla**

Hebron is a classic case of the metaphor of resistance.

**Zaha Hadid**

We haven't had a real consensus since the beginning, and this makes our decisions kind of fragmented. Some people have an interest in architecture; others are interested in so-called politically correct projects, some people are anti-form. I think the problem with all of these projects is that they all look a bit dated. It's easy to like the Lepers Hospital or the renovation projects because they don't have a date to them. The rest are dated. They lack freshness. I feel like I've seen these things a hundred times before, since I was a student. I am not saying these are invalid projects. Personally, I am against restoration because it takes away from invention. People should have the confidence to build new things with the same strength as has been done historically. There was an excitement, for example, in the last cycle when Ken Yeang's tower in Kuala Lumpur was chosen. It had relevance for the rest of the world. People could relate to it.

**Saleh Al-Hathloul**

But one can actually use the argument of history, if a history is being lost, to preserve something that represents the past. When something important remains, it deserves to be looked at or preserved in order for future generations to see what came before.

# The Aga Khan Award as

Following the creation of the Aga Khan Award for Architecture, a seminar called 'Architecture in the Spirit of Islam' was held in April 1978 at Aiglemont, just north of Paris. The participants debated passionately on issues that have recurred in all of the ensuing seminars organized by the Award, as well as in the discussions among the members of the Award's successive Steering Committees and Master Juries for the past 20 years. When he founded the Award, the Aga Khan had the vision of a forum for research, study and critical analysis of the new historical problems facing Muslim societies in the first decades of their independence. He wanted to offer a space for free debate to all interested parties to identify the conditions, the ways, the obstacles and the actions related to the conservation, restoration, improvement and creation of the built environment in historical cities and, more generally, in all spaces designed for contemporary Muslim societies.

During the 1980s, international relations were driven by the cold war between the 'free world' and the 'communist world'; the 'Third World' – as we called the rest of the world before November 1989 – had to seek help and protection from one or the other of the big two. Muslim societies were torn between the will to restore their 'Islamic identity' and the idea of 'scientific socialism', which was presented as the best revolutionary political programme to emancipate underdeveloped societies from the domination of capitalism. This ideological debate imposed a conceptual frame, a social and historical *imaginaire*, strongly polarized between tradition and modernity, conservation and progress, development and underdevelopment, domination and emancipation, liberal capitalism and socialist collectivism, and so forth. Architecture became an excellent channel for dispensing with ideological polemics, exploring concrete issues and deepening consideration of urgent problems in culture, the environment and the urban fabric in societies deprived for centuries of human, scientific and material resources.

The most talented and successful architects in the world have contributed to the Award as a thinking process, as members either of the Master Jury or of the Steering Committee; they have exchanged and discussed cultural, historical and anthropological aspects of architecture and urban fabrics in Islamic contexts with specialists in the social sciences who have neither the experience of the architects nor always the required critical approach to Islam as a religion, a cultural tradition, a system of thought. A significant number of architects, however, have often had a very superficial knowledge not only about what I call Islamic contexts – including expressions of classical as well as contemporary Islam – but also, and more essentially, about problems related to religious architecture in general, Islam being just a case study among others.

His Highness long ago expressed his wish to devote more critical thinking to the problems of faith, spirituality and ethics as applied to the architectural design of buildings specifically devoted to religious life (mosques, mausoleums, pilgrimage facilities).

# a Process of Thinking

Mohammed Arkoun

We discovered then the difficulties related to the spirit of education in schools of architecture: the contents of the programmes and the weakness in or total lack of cross-disciplinary or cross-cultural approaches in the teaching of architecture. When we speak of programmes, methodologies, problematics, levels of thinking and horizons of meaning in architectural teaching, we refer exclusively to Western schools and professors; the most famous and successful architects who originate from the Islamic world are trained in the spirit, techniques and cultural and intellectual frames prevailing in the modern Western tradition. As a historian of Islamic thought, I have observed time and again that several – not all, fortunately – so-called 'Muslim' architects and planners are as far from or indifferent to the problems of interface between religion and architecture as their Western colleagues.

I am not at all defending the romantic, contemplative posture of those who repeat conventional, uncritical positions on an architecture 'in the spirit of Islam'. I have always shown a radical criticism against those – architects, Islamicists, theologians, politicians, average Muslims – who reduce Islamic characteristics to the presence of traditional forms like the minaret, dome, *muqarnas, mashrabiyya,* tent, rules of privacy and the like. These elements have become mere *signals* and have lost all of their old symbolic value in the contemporary designed environment. Even in Western contexts, many mosques have been built without any effort to propose new forms or new combinations that would integrate the rich expectations made explicit in the interfaith dialogues since the 1960s. In several oral and written interventions, I have insisted on the important differences between *signals, signs* and *symbols* in semiotic analysis. Art criticism in general has been enriched by the well-known theory of *aesthetics of reception* developed decades ago by the Frankfurt School. The critical evaluation of a work of art – poem, novel, monument, temple, symphony, painting, sculpture, garden, landscape – cannot be made by focusing only on the author and his intentions; we know that each user or receiver rewrites or reinterprets the piece according to his or her own values and system of connotations. Accordingly, there is a constant interactive transformation of the signals, signs, symbols and metaphors as used by the author and received by the reader-interpreter of each semiotic composition. When architects look for 'excellence', however, they care less about the *aesthetics of reception* and more about the design as it is taught, learned and reproduced among the leading practitioners.

When all of these considerations about a more radical, semiotic, historical, sociological and anthropological criticism are introduced in the discussions among members of the Steering Committee or the Master Jury, the search for the inclusive, exhaustive approach of architecture in Islamic contexts ends abruptly with the simple

MOHAMMED ARKOUN

153

Darb Qirmiz Quarter

Restoration of Bukhara Old City

so with the integrated treatment and improvement of the natural environment within a major urban centre. The water in the city's two rivers and reservoirs was seriously polluted, contaminated by sewage from all over Indore. The slum networking programme introduced sewerage systems in most of the city's 183 slums, and a purification system and process that returns the treated water into the rivers. The rivers themselves are now the vital centre of the city, enhanced by landscaping of the river banks to create public parks and pedestrian walkways.

Another concern of the Award in urban areas is the protection and revitalization of historic districts which, in most of our cities, have sadly deteriorated. Each cycle of the Award has brought forward examples of novel approaches to the social, economic and cultural problems which the old city centres face, as well as to architectural deterioration. The successive Award juries have awarded two types of approaches to urban conservation efforts. One has focused on individual buildings restored architecturally to accommodate new programmes, usually cultural or social centres, in order to re-establish them as poles of community activity within the historical fabric. In addition to this social purpose, they also very often have served as demonstration projects, providing restoration, renovation and rehabilitation techniques to the residents of the old city.

*Darb Qirmiz Quarter, Cairo, Egypt, 1983*
*Historic Sites Development, Istanbul, Turkey, 1986*
*Palace Parks Programme, Istanbul, Turkey, 1992*
*Kairouan Conservation Programme, Tunisia, 1992*

The other approach to historic environments has been a more integrated one that addresses the built fabric of entire districts, one that brings architectural restoration together with programmes for social development and economic sustainability.

*Sidi Bou Saïd, Tunis, Tunisia, 1980*
*Mostar Old Town, Bosnia-Herzegovina, 1986*
*Rehabilitation of Asilah, Morocco, 1989*
*Conservation of Old Sana'a, Yemen, 1992*
*Restoration of Bukhara Old City, Uzbekistan, 1995*

This second approach is particularly evident in another winning project in this cycle, the Rehabilitation of Hebron Old Town, the heroic undertaking of dedicated resi-

Medical Centre

Gürel Family Summer Residence

dents to revitalize the abandoned, dilapidated, almost-dead old town of Hebron. It is now
healthy, living and vibrant, as if there had been no hiatus in its existence. Hebron has had
critical problems concerning politics, finance, etc., but the rehabilitation is so successful
it is as if there were never any of these difficulties. The project in Hebron is the culmina-
tion of the efforts of those who wish to re-establish a dialogue with their past by means
of their architectural heritage. In today's world, given adversity and political differences
and the struggle for historical continuity and cultural identity, this project carries an
important message for the world at large about what peace can bring to troubled
areas everywhere.

The Award has yet to be given to modern, integrated hospitals, although two health
facilities, in Mali and Mauritania, have been characterized by architectural innovation that
creatively employs local technology and materials while responding to specific needs.

*Medical Centre, Mopti, Mali, 1980*
*Kaedi Regional Hospital, Kaedi, Mauritania, 1995*

Likewise, in this cycle, the Lepers Hospital in India is the work of two young Norwegian volunteer architects whose efforts contributed to alleviating the social circumstances
and physical pain of an ancient disease. They harnessed local skills to create an architectural setting for the peace and comfort of patients who, because of their illness, are cast out
by society. The building symbolizes the hope of architecture to serve all people.

Throughout the history of architecture, private houses have provided fertile
ground for the expression and development of architectural excellence, and have often
been featured in various cycles of the Award; here, too, social consciousness has played
an important role in the private houses selected by the Award.

*Halawa House, Agamy, Egypt, 1980*
*Ertegün House, Bodrum, Turkey, 1980*
*Nail Çakirhan House, Akyaka Village, Turkey, 1983*
*Gürel Family Summer Residence, Çanakkale, Turkey, 1989*

In this cycle, the jury selected the Salinger Residence in Malaysia as an important
expression of the reinterpretation of traditional Malay architecture and craftsmanship
in a contemporary fashion, which serves a client who values traditional culture and protection of the environment.

SUHA ÖZKAN

Sherefudin's White Mosque

Landmark achievements in contemporary architecture have also had a prominent place in each cycle of Award recipients, though, again, always with specific symbolic, historical and climatic relevance to local context.

*Water Towers, Kuwait City, Kuwait, 1980*
*Inter-Continental Hotel and Conference Centre, Mecca, Saudi Arabia, 1980*
*Sherefudin's White Mosque, Visoko, Bosnia-Herzegovina, 1983*
*Hajj Terminal, King Abdul Aziz International Airport, Jeddah, Saudi Arabia, 1983*
*National Assembly Building, Sher-e-Bangla Nagar, Dhaka, Bangladesh, 1989*
*Ministry of Foreign Affairs, Riyadh, Saudi Arabia, 1989*
*Mosque of the Grand National Assembly, Ankara, Turkey, 1995*
*Menara Mesiniaga, Kuala Lumpur, Malaysia, 1995*

Three projects represent this tradition in this cycle: the Alhamra Arts Council in Lahore, Pakistan; Vidhan Bhavan in Bhopal, India; and Tuwaiq Palace in Riyadh, Saudi Arabia. Together and individually, they demonstrate the vibrancy and high calibre of contemporary architecture in Muslim societies.

In the Alhamra Arts Council, Nayyar Ali Dada establishes a fortress-like compound that opens itself to the public of Lahore via art, theatre and performance. The indoor and outdoor spaces provide for a variety of activities and performances; as importantly, it provides for and encourages social interaction in a popular, public fashion. The extensive use of red brick refers to examples of Mughal architecture, yet the architect makes no compromise to regional derivation or expressionism and instead employs a free-form vocabulary characterized by angular geometries.

Vidhan Bhavan houses the regional parliament of Madhya Pradesh State, and the architect, Charles Correa, has created a complex to symbolize government as the voice, expression and plurality of society. By employing a circle as the generating form of the complex, he has emphasized unity and continuity and, within it, has created an architectural variety to express harmony and diversity. The plan draws on various layers of Islamic, Buddhist and Hindu architectures and histories, and masterfully combines them, introducing mythological patterns and symbolism along with the architect's own free expression. Contemporary artists from throughout Madhya Pradesh were brought in to contribute their own works, thus adding yet another layer of expression to the already rich complex. The interior spaces, which accommodate government assemblies and administrative offices, are married to a variety of courtyards, again reflecting Correa's long commitment to the natural environment and his focus on spaces 'open to the sky'.

Water Towers

Menara Mesiniaga

Tuwaiq Palace draws inspiration from the natural environment and arid desert climate in Saudi Arabia. The winding, rampart-like exterior walls contain all of the programmatic functions and serve to protect a lush man-made oasis at the project's centre. The austere, stone-clad exterior is penetrated by a few small openings, similar to traditional Najdi structures. Large, tensile structures protrude from the outside, recalling nomad tents, another expression of Saudi culture.

## Continuity and Evolution of the Award

In their selection of seven winning projects and in their deliberations, the 1998 Master Jury paid particular attention to the continuity and ongoing process of the Award programme, and specifically refrained from the selection of projects that represented trends, messages or statements that had been made in the past. They did not feel that it was necessary to define categories or themes of expression, since they believe that each of the seven winning projects speaks clearly for itself, and conveys a *universal* message with eloquence and poignancy.

Past juries have sometimes developed thematic contexts in which to view the projects that have been selected for Awards. The first jury, in 1980, conceived of the Award as an ongoing search, and identified fifteen winning projects in seven categories. The 1983, 1986 and 1989 Master Juries again emphasized the notion of a process and ongoing search, but in 1992 the jury attempted to formulate specific directions or distinct categories within which the winning projects might be seen. The nine winning projects were grouped in two categories, 'Enhancing Urban Environments' and 'Generating New Architectural Languages'. The projects themselves revealed the same concerns as in earlier cycles, including social housing and community improvement, revitalization and protection of the historical architectural fabric and achievements in contemporary architectural design.

In 1995 the jury gave even further importance to the role and importance of architecture as a medium of communication in a global context. They used the themes of 'Critical Social Discourse', 'Critical Architectural and Urbanistic Discourse' and 'Innovative Concepts' to develop and present the eleven winning projects they selected. The 1995 jury also gave particular importance to broadening the participation in and access to the Award programme, and made the unprecedented gesture of requesting portions of their recorded deliberations to be published. The series of books published at the end of each cycle have always provided an additional forum for critical thinking on the topics of architecture and society. The titles, all within the series 'Building in the Islamic World Today', reveal the evolution of the Award over the past two decades.

*Architecture and Community (1980)*
*Architecture in Continuity (1983)*
*Space for Freedom: The Search for Architectural Excellence in Muslim Societies (1986)*
*Architecture for Islamic Societies Today (1989)*
*Architecture for a Changing World (1992)*
*Architecture beyond Architecture: Creativity and Social Transformations in Islamic Cultures (1995)*

SUHA ÖZKAN

# Project Data and Personnel

## Rehabilitation of Hebron Old Town

| | |
|---|---|
| *Client* | Hebron Rehabilitation Committee, Ali Kawasmi, Chairman |
| *Planners/ Conservators* | Engineering Office of the Hebron Rehabilitation Committee, Khalid Fahed Qawasmi, Resident Engineer. Administration: Emad Hamdan, Administrative Manager; Mohammed Al-Sharif and Mohammad Al-Jaabari, Executive Managers; Tawfeeq Jahshen, Lawyer; Nuha Abu Sara, Social Researcher. Technical Team: Hilmi Maraqa, Tahsseen Al-Natsheh, and Hisham Zaloom, Civil Engineers; Abdel Qader Al-Sharabati, Architectural Engineer; Hamed Al-Karakee, Ibraheem Diab Hasan, Ismaeel Abd Al Rahman, Fakhri Abu Zina, Ibraheem Sadeq, Riad Al-Qazaqi, Waleed Al-Homoz, Mohammed Abu Zunade, Fayez Abu Mukadam, Bassam Hassonah, and Yakoub Al-Natsheh, Site Supervisors; Samar Badar, Architectural Draftsman |
| *Consultants* | Hebron University Graduates Union, Ahmad Said Tamimi, President; Ibrahim Amro, Secretary General; Ghassan Aldwaik, Civil Engineer. Al-Aqsa Rehilitation Committee, Isam Awwad. Welfare Organisation, Shadia Toquan. Ministry of Tourism, Hamdan Taha, Archeaologist. Riwaq, Suad Amiri, Director; Nami Al-Joubi, Co-Director. Nuha Dandis, Architectural Engineer. Farouq Yaghmor, Architect |
| *Sponsors* | Islamic Development Bank; Arab Fund for Economic & Social Development, Kuwait. |
| *Studies and Documentation* | 1988–1992 |
| *Restoration* | August 1995 and ongoing |
| *Occupation* | September 1995 and ongoing |
| *Site Area* | approx. 270,000 m² |
| *Built area* | approx. 160,000 m² |
| *Rehabilitated area* | 127 dwellings and 25 shops restored by 1998; work is going on in 95 other buildings |
| *Cost* | US $3,000,000 (up to May 1998) |

### Hebron Rehabilitation Committee (HRC)

Established as a result of the decision by the President of the Palestinian Authority, Mr Yasser Arafat, to rehabilitate and upgrade the old stone town of Hebron. HRC has thirteen members, including the Minister of Transportation, officials from the Ministry of Sports and Ministry of Waqf and representatives from NGOs. These members chair lower committees which are responsible for issues relating to housing, tender, public relations, purchasing, legal issues, information and social welfare. The executive arm of HRC is the Engineering Office, which performs the function of the town planning office. It has two main divisions, an administration office and a technical office that staffs the projects and controls their implementation.

## Slum Networking of Indore City, India

| | |
|---|---|
| *Client* | Indore Development Authority: Chandrashekhar M. Dagaonkar, Director of Indore Habitat Improvement Project; M.L. Bhatt, former Project Director; Dilip Agashe, Executive Engineer; Vijay Marathe, Assistant Engineer; V.V. Apte, Technical Assistant |
| *Planners* | Himanshu H. Parikh Consulting Engineers: Himanshu H. Parikh, Civil Engineer; Priti Parikh, Project Engineer |
| *Consultant* | Chetan Engineers & Surveyors |
| *Funding and Monitoring* | United Kingdom Overseas Development Administration |
| *Commission* | March 1989 |
| *Design* | 1987–1995 |
| *Construction* | 1989 and ongoing |
| *Occupation* | 1989 and ongoing |
| *Number of slums* | 183 |
| *Total slum area* | 800–1000 hectares |
| *Number of households covered* | 80,000 |
| *Population covered* | over 500,000 |
| *Cost* | INR 600,000,000 (US $15,600,000) |

### Himanshu Parikh

Graduated from Cambridge University, where he obtained both his bachelor's and master's degrees in engineering sciences with honours. In 1982 Mr Parikh established Himanshu Parikh Consulting Engineers in Ahmedabad, India. The practice offers consultancy services in urban planning, infrastructure design and environmental upgrading, with an emphasis on urban low-income areas. He has held various positions outside his practice, including professor at the school of planning, Centre for Environmental Planning and Technology in Ahmedabad, and visiting lecturer at the Human Settlements Management Institute in Delhi. Mr Parikh has been the recipient of several awards including the Fazlur Khan International Travelling Fellowship for excellence in structural engineering in 1985, the United Nations World Habitat Award for Urban Development in 1993, and the Habitat II Best Practice recognition for Slum Networking in 1996.

## Lepers Hospital, Chopda Taluka, India

| | |
|---|---|
| Client | Norwegian Free Evangelical Mission, India Trust: Pastor Vijay Sapkale, Mission-Incharge; Clara and Leif Lerberg, Mission Representatives |
| Architects | Per Christian Brynildsen and Jan Olav Jensen |
| Consultants | Terje Orlien and Kristoffer Apeland, Structural Engineers |
| Contractor | N. Sampatt |
| Sponsors | Norwegian Agency for Development Co-operation (NORAD); Hope 82 Charity Campaign |
| Commission | March 1983 |
| Design | April 1983–September 1984 |
| Construction | June 1983–May 1985 |
| Occupation | July 1985 |
| Site Area | 8,000 m² |
| Built area | 1,000 m² |
| Cost | IRP 1,400,000 (US $140,000) |

### Per Christian Brynildsen and Jan Olav Jensen

Norwegian architects who attended the Oslo School of Architecture and graduated in 1985 and 1986 respectively. In March 1983, Messrs Jensen and Brynildsen travelled to India, where they were asked by two Norwegian missionaries to prepare a design for the Lepers Hospital in Chopda. In 1995 Mr Jensen established his own architectural firm, Jensen & Skodvin Arkitektkontor. He has been a visiting critic at several schools including Trondheim University in Norway, and in 1998 was the Kenzo Tange Visiting Design Critic at the Graduate School of Design at Harvard University. Mr Brynildsen has taught at the Oslo School of Architecture and the Bergen School of Architecture in Norway and has lectured both in Norway and Sweden. He currently concentrates on residential projects in Norway.

## Salinger Residence, Selangor, Malaysia

| | |
|---|---|
| Clients | Rudin and Munira Salinger |
| Architect | CSL Associates: Jimmy Lim Cheok Siang, Principal; Raymond Siew Ching Ng, Draftsman |
| Craftsman | Ibrahim bin Adam, Master Carpenter |
| Commission | August 1984 |
| Design | June 1985–October 1985 |
| Construction | February 1986–June 1992 |
| Occupation | July 1992 |
| Site Area | 12,140 m² |
| Built area | 289 m² |
| Cost | MRP 280,000 (US $112,000) |

### Jimmy C.S. Lim

Malaysian architect who established CSL Associates in 1978 after having practised for ten years, five of which were spent in Australia, where he had graduated from the University of New South Wales. Mr Lim's work is characterized by its response to the climate and environment and his ongoing search to define a national character for Malaysian architecture. He has been actively involved in the Malaysian Institute of Architects (PAM), both as a member and as its president. Mr Lim is interested in conservation issues and was a founding member of the Friends of Heritage of Malaysia and the director of the Heritage Trust of Malaysia. Mr Lim has received several awards including the Commonwealth Association of Architects National Award in 1985, an award for the use of timber in building from the Malaysian Timber Industry Board in 1988 and the Norway Award for Outstanding Contribution to Quality in 1991.

## Tuwaiq Palace, Riyadh, Saudi Arabia

| | |
|---|---|
| Client | Arriyadh Development Authority: Muhammad bin Abdul-Aziz Al-Shaikh, Former President; Abdellatif Al-Shaikh, President |
| Architects | OHO Joint Venture: Atelier Frei Otto, Büro Happold and Omrania. Omrania Architects, Planners, and Engineers: Basem Shihabi and Nabil Fanous, Principals; Ward Thompson, Project Manager; Norman Lingwood, Senior Architect; Kilic Uyanik, Urban Designer; Stefan Schlau and Richard Buchanan, Senior Architects; Pauline McComb, Senior Landscape Architect; Richard Stone, Landscape Architect; Alan Cartwright, Interior Design. Atelier Frei Otto: Frei Otto, Principal; Johannes Fritz, Project Architect; H. Doster, Architect. Büro Happold: Edmond Happold, Principal; Terry Ealey, Project Engineer; Roger Webster, Project Coordinator; David Mumby, Senior Services Engineer; Ian Liddell, Special Structures; Mick Green, Design Engineer; Tony McLaughlin, Services Engineer; Vincent Grant, Civil Engineer. Site Management Team: J.W.E. Pugh, Project Manager; D. Rhys-Jones, Scheduler; C. J. Craig, Senior Architect; E.H.W. Cook, Quality Control Supervisor; W.J. Finn, Materials & Civil Engineer; P.A. McLaughlin, Mechanical Engineer; P. Kelly, Structural Engineer; R. Hafeli, Architect; P. Rees, Electrical Engineer; R. Stone, Landscape Architect |
| Contractor | Hanyang Corporation |
| Competition | March 1980 |
| Design | June 1981–January 1983 |
| Construction | April 1983–December 1984 |
| Occupation | December 1985 |
| Site Area | 75,000 m² |
| Built area | 24,000 m² |
| Cost | SAR 117,000,000 (US $31,200,000) |

### OHO Joint Venture: Atelier Frei Otto, Büro Happold and Omrania

Created in 1980 for a one-time endeavour that combined two entries of a limited architecture competition submitted by Omrania Architects and Atelier Frei Otto with the structural engineering firm Büro Happold. Omrania Architects, Planners and Engineers, was established in 1973 by Messrs Basem Al-Shihabi and Nabil Fanous in Riyadh, Saudi Arabia, and has undertaken town planning, architecture and project management throughout the Middle East. Frei Otto is a pioneer in the building of modern tensile architecture. His innovations in form, materials, structure and testing techniques have earned him numerous awards, including the Aga Khan Award for Architecture in 1980, the International Design Award in 1982, the Honda Prize in 1990 and the Wekbund Preis in 1992. Mr Otto has lectured and taught at many institutions in Germany and abroad. The late Edmund Happold established Büro Happold when he left Ove Arup & Partners to direct the School of Architecture and Engineering in Bath, England, in 1976. The office specializes in light, inflatable and suspended structures. Büro Happold has collaborated with many renowned architects including Renzo Piano and Richard Rogers.

## Alhamra Arts Council, Lahore, Pakistan

| | |
|---|---|
| Client | Lahore Arts Council:  Shahbaz Sharif, Chief Minister of Punjab, Patron-in-Chief; Khawaja Mohammad Naeem, Chairman |
| Architect | Nayyar Ali Dada and Associates:  Nayyar Ali Dada, Principal Designer, Tenveer Hasan and Ghazanfar Ali, Assistant Architects |
| Consultants | Shahid Hameed, Structural Engineering; Mohammad Ibrar, Electrical Engineering |
| Contractors | Builders Associates Ltd., Masud H. Siddiqui (Phases I & II); AFCO Builders Ltd., Sami Khan |

**Phase I**

| | |
|---|---|
| Commission | July 1969 |
| Design | January 1973–November 1974 |
| Construction | July 1975–September 1979 |
| Occupation | December 1979 |

**Phase II**

| | |
|---|---|
| Commission | March 1980 |
| Design | April 1980 |
| Construction | August 1982–November 1983 |
| Occupation | December 1983 |

**Phase III**

| | |
|---|---|
| Commission | June 1983 |
| Design | September 1983 |
| Construction | Decembre 1983–May 1985 |
| Occupation | July 1985 |

**Phase IV**

| | |
|---|---|
| Commission | February 1989 |
| Design | May 1989 |
| Construction | April 1990–March 1992 |
| Occupation | September 1992 |
| Site Area | 16,730 m² |
| Built area | 13,848 m² |
| Cost | PKR 57,000,000 (US $1,965,000) |

### Nayyar Ali Dada

Pakistani architect whose numerous works have been recognized both at home and abroad. He pioneered the cause of conservation in Pakistan, and is a founding member of the Lahore Conservation Society. Mr Dada is devoted to the education of young architects, and has been a lecturer at Lahore's National College of Arts since 1965; he was named a Fellow of the College in 1976. Mr Dada is actively involved in the creative arts in Pakistan, both as watercolourist and as the director of a private gallery, and is a board member of and adviser to many cultural institutions. In 1992 Mr Dada was presented with the President's Pride of Performance Award for his services to Pakistan.

## Vidhan Bhavan, Bhopal, India

| | |
|---|---|
| Client | State Government of Madhya Pradesh:  Shri Digvijay Singh, Chief Minister of Madhya Pradesh; Mahesh N. Buch, Chairman, Empowered Committee; Probir Sen, Secretary of Housing |
| Architect | Charles Correa.  Project Team: Hema Sankalia, Nidish Majmundar, Suneel Shelar, Andrew Fernandes, Rahul Mehrotra, Viren Ahuja, and Manoj Shetty |
| Consultants | Mahendra Raj, Structural Engineering; S. K. Murthy, Mechanical Engineering; Gautam Suri, Acoustics; Satish Madhiwala, Interior Design; Kishore Pradhan, Landscape Architecture; Kirti Tridevi, Graphic Design |
| Artwork | Yogesh Rawal, Gulam Sheikh, Robin David, Tushar Dighe and Jangarh Singh |
| Contractor | M/s Sood & Sood |
| Commission | July 1982 |
| Design | July 1982–July 1984 |
| Construction | September 1982–January 1996 |
| Occupation | August 1993 |
| Site Area | 85,000 m² |
| Built area | 32,000 m² |
| Cost | IRP 408,000,000 (US $11,530,000) |

### Charles Correa

Indian architect, planner, activist and theoretician who studied architecture at the Massachusetts Institute of Technology (MIT) and the University of Michigan. He has taught and lectured at many universities, both in India and abroad, including MIT, Harvard University, the University of London and Cambridge University, where he was Nehru Professor. Mr Correa is known for the wide range of his architectural work in India and on urbanization and low-cost shelter in the Third World, which he articulated in his 1985 publication 'The New Landscape'. His architectural designs have been internationally acclaimed and he has received many awards, including the Royal Institute of British Architects Gold Medal in 1984, the Indian Institute of Architects Gold Medal in 1987, the International Union of Architects Gold Medal in 1990 and the Praemium Imperiale for Architecture from the Japan Art Association in 1994.

# The 1998 Award Steering Committee

### His Highness The Aga Khan, Chairman

### Selma Al-Radi

Iraqi archaeologist and a research associate at New York University. She has worked in Yemen since 1977. In 1983 she undertook the restoration of the sixteenth-century Madrasa Al-Amiryah in the town of Rada', and currently she is overseeing the final phase of the project, including the restoration of the internal wall paintings. She is also now completing the rehabilitation of the complex of Imamate palaces at the National Museum in Sana'a, Yemen, and preparing a catalogue of the museum's collections for publication. Dr Al-Radi has excavated sites in Iraq, Egypt, Kuwait, Cyprus, Syria and Yemen, and has published in Arabic and English. She was a member of the 1986 and 1995 Award Technical Reviews and of the 1989 and 1992 Steering Committees.

### Balkrishna V. Doshi

Indian architect, educator and academic. After initial study in Bombay, he worked with Le Corbusier in Paris (1951–54) as senior designer, and then in India to supervise Corbusier's projects in Ahmedabad and Chandigarh. Professor Doshi established the Vastu-Shilpa Foundation for Studies and Research in Environmental Design in 1955, known for pioneering work in low-cost housing and city planning. Today, his internationally renowned projects are designed under the name of Vastu-Shilpa Consultants, with offices in Ahmedabad. As an academic, Professor Doshi has been visiting the USA and Europe since 1958, and has held important chairs in American universities. He has received numerous international awards and honours, including Padma Shri from the Government of India and an honorary doctorate from the University of Pennsylvania. Professor Doshi served a member of the 1992 Award Master Jury and was presented with a 1995 Aga Khan Award for Architecture for the Aranya Community Housing in Indore, India.

### Peter Eisenman

American architect and educator. He is the Irwin S. Chanin Distinguished Professor at The Cooper Union in New York City and the principal of Eisenman Architects. Among his built projects are the Wexner Centre for the Arts and Fine Arts Library at Ohio State University in Columbus, completed in 1989, and a project for social housing at Checkpoint Charlie in Berlin. He has built two office buildings in Tokyo, a convention centre in Columbus, Ohio, and the Aronoff Centre for Design and Art in Cincinnati, Ohio. Mr Eisenman was the founder and director of the Institute for Architecture and Urban Studies, an international think-tank for architectural ideas, from 1967 to 1980. Mr Eisenman served as a member of the 1995 Award Master Jury.

### Charles Jencks

American architect and architectural historian, is well known as the critic who first defined post-modernism in architecture, an event which led to its subsequent definition in many fields. A visiting professor at the University of California at Los Angeles, he is the author of many books on architecture and culture, including *The Language of Post-Modern Architecture* (6th edn, 1981), *What is Post-Modernism?* (4th edn, 1996) and *The Architecture of the Jumping Universe* (1995). His recent work is on cosmogonic architecture and complexity theory. He lectures widely in the United States, Japan and Europe, has made a number of television programmes on architecture and designed important objects, including buildings, furniture and landscape gardens. Professor Jencks served as a member of the 1995 Award Master Jury.

### Adhi Moersid

Indonesian architect in private practice with PT Atelier 6 Architects, where he is actively involved in the design, planning and construction of Atelier 6 projects, and senior vice-president of Atelier 6 Holding Company. Mr Moersid has been honorary chairman of the Indonesian Institute of Architects since 1989, and was deputy chairman of ARCASIA (Architects Regional Council Asia) from 1987 to 1989. He was a lecturer in the School of Design at the Jakarta Institute of Arts from 1970 to 1980, and continues to be an external examiner for several schools of architecture. In 1986 Mr Moersid received an Honourable Mention from the Aga Khan Award for Architecture for the Saïd Naum Mosque in Jakarta. During the 1992 Award cycle, he served as a member of the Award Master Jury.

### Luis Monreal

Spanish historian, is currently director general of the Caixa Foundation in Barcelona. From 1985 to 1990 he was the director of the Getty Conservation Institute and oversaw conservation of projects such as the Tomb of Nefertari in Upper Egypt, the Sphinx in Giza and Buddhist temples in Mogao (Datong, China), as well as other major projects in Cyprus, Jordan, Cambodia and Spain. Mr Monreal was the secretary general of the International Council of Museums (ICOM) from 1974 to 1985, and responsible for the establishment or conservation of nine museums throughout the world. He has also served as the curator of the Marés Museum in Barcelona, and was a professor of the history of art and museology at the Autonomous University of Barcelona. Mr Monreal has participated in numerous archaeological expeditions, to the High Atlas Mountains (Morocco), Nubia, Abkanarti (Sudan) and Masmas (Egypt). He was a member of the 1995 Award Master Jury.

### Azim Nanji

Born in Nairobi, Kenya, attended schools in Kenya and Tanzania and Makerere University in Uganda, and received his master's and doctoral degrees in Islamic Studies from McGill University. He has taught at both Canadian and American universities and was the Margaret Gest Professor for the Cross-Cultural Study of Religion at Haverford College, Pennsylvania. He is currently professor and chair of the Department of Religion at the University of Florida at Gainesville. Dr Nanji is co-chair of the

Islam Section at the American Academy of Religion and a member of the Council of the Foundations Committee on Religions and Philanthropy. In 1995 Dr Nanji was invited to deliver the baccalaureate address at Stanford University's convocation ceremonies. He served as a member of the Master Jury of the 1992 Aga Khan Award for Architecture and edited a monograph on the Award entitled *Building for Tomorrow*, published by Academy Editions (1994).

### Ali Shuaibi

Saudi Arabian architect and planner, is a co-founder of Beeah Planners, Architects and Engineers, based in Riyadh, with projects in Saudi Arabia, Oman, Yemen, Pakistan and Djibouti. Mr Shuaibi teaches design at King Saud University, and is co-editor of the *Urban Heritage Encyclopaedia*. Several of his projects have received national and international awards, including the Al-Kindi Plaza at Hayy Assafarat, the diplomatic quarter in Riyadh, which received an Aga Khan Award for Architecture in 1989 and the Architectural Project Award of the Organization of Arab Towns in 1990. With Beeah, he is currently at work on the National Museum in Riyadh, the Institute of Public Administration in Jeddah and the Embassy of Saudi Arabia in Tunis. Mr Shuaibi was a member of the 1992 Award Master Jury and the 1995 Award Steering Committee.

# The 1998 Master Jury

### Mohammed Arkoun

French academician of Algerian origin, is Emeritus Professor of the History of Islamic Thought at the Sorbonne (Paris III), and visiting professor at universities in the United States, Europe and the Muslim world. Professor Arkoun's work and interests concentrate on classical Islam and contemporary issues of slam facing modernity. He is associated with several European initiatives to rethink and reshape the relationship between Europe, Islam and the Mediterranean world, and is the author of numerous publications, including *L'Humanisme arabe au IVe/Xe siècle* (1982), *Pour une critique de la raison islamique* (1984), *Arab Thought* (1988), and *Rethinking Islam: Common Questions – Uncommon Answers* (1993). Professor Arkoun served as a member of the Award Steering Committee from 1983 to 1992, and as a member of the 1995 Award Master Jury. He was decorated as an Officer of the French Legion of Honour in July 1996.

### Zaha Hadid

London-based architectural designer whose work encompasses all fields of design, ranging from large-scale urbanism to products, interiors, and furniture. Ms Hadid studied architecture at the Architectural Association (AA), London, where she was awarded the Diploma Prize in 1977. She then joined the Office of

Metropolitan Architecture (OMA) and began teaching at the Architectural Association with OMA collaborators Rem Koolhaas and Elia Zenghleis; she later led her own studio at the AA until 1987. Her work was awarded wide international recognition in 1983 with her winning entry for the Hong Kong Peak Competition. This was followed by first-place awards for competitions in Kurfürstendamm, Berlin (1986); for an Art and Media Centre in Düsseldorf (1989); and for the Cardiff Bay Opera House (1994). In 1993 Ms Hadid's fire station for the Vitra furniture company opened to much public acclaim. Her IBA housing scheme in Berlin was completed the same year. Ms Hadid's paintings and drawings are an important testing field for her ideas. They have been widely published and exhibited, in the 'Deconstructivist Architecture' show at the Museum of Modern Art in New York (1988), the Graduate School of Design at Harvard University (1995) and the San Francisco Museum of Modern Art (1998). Her work was also featured in the Master's Section of the 1996 Venice Biennale. In 1996 Ms Hadid was shortlisted as a finalist for the Victoria and Albert Museum's new Boilerhouse Gallery in London and for a Philharmonique in Luxembourg; her office is also joint winner of the Thames Water Habitable Bridge competition. Current work includes a housing scheme in Vienna and projects in London. Ms Hadid was awarded the Sullivan Chair for 1997 at the University of Illinois, Chicago, school of architecture, and a guest professorship at the Hochschule für Bildende Künste in Hamburg, also in 1997.

### Saleh Al-Hathloul

Saudi Arabian educator and a critic in the field of architecture, with interests in epistemology, structural changes in society and futurist studies. He received a master's degree in urban design from Harvard University (1975) and a PhD in architecture from the Massachusetts Institute of Technology (1981). He was an assistant professor and chair of the department of architecture at King Saud University in Riyadh from 1981 to 1984, and chairman of the board of Al-Umran (the Saudi Arabian Society for Architects and Planners) from its inception in 1989 until 1993. Dr Al-Hathloul served as a jury member of the Award of the Organization of Arab Cities for the past three cycles. He is the author of numerous books and articles on planning and architecture, of which *The Arab Muslim City* (1994) is the best known. Since 1984 Dr Al-Hathloul has been the deputy minister for town planning, Ministry of Municipal and Rural Affairs, Kingdom of Saudi Arabia, with the responsibility of directing and supervising all national, regional and local planning in the kingdom.

### Arif Hasan

Pakistani architect and planner, teacher, social researcher and writer, studied architecture at the Oxford Polytechnic, England, from 1960 to 1965, and established an independent architecture practice in Karachi in 1968. He has been a consultant to various United Nations agencies, international organizations, non-governmental organizations and community groups both in the North and South. Mr Hasan is renowned for his involvement with low-income settlement programmes and is the architect of a large number of important residential, commercial and educational facilities in Pakistan. The Orangi Pilot Project to which he is consultant has attracted international attention and in 1990 the Japanese government presented Mr Hasan with its International Year for the Shelterless Memorial Award. Mr Hasan served as a member of the 1992 and 1995 Award Steering Committees and as a member of the 1989 Award Technical Review.

## Arata Isozaki

Japanese architect, was educated at the University of Tokyo, Faculty of Architecture. He worked with Kenzo Tange's Team and Urtec, Tokyo, from 1954 to 1963, when he established his own practice, the Arata Isozaki Atelier. Mr Isozaki's major buildings include the Museum of Contemporary Art in Los Angeles (1986), the Sant Jordi Sports Palace for the Olympic Games in Barcelona (1990), Art Tower Mito in Ibaragi (1990), the Team Disney Building in Buena Vista, Florida (1991), Domus: La Casa del Hombre in La Coruña, Spain (1995) and the Kyoto Concert Hall (1995). His work has been widely published and exhibited and he has received numerous awards and honours, including three Annual Prizes of the Japan Architectural Association, the *Interiors* Award (1983) and the Gold Medal of the Royal Institute of British Architects (1986). Mr Isozaki is an Honorary Fellow of the American Institute of Architects (1983), of the Bund Deutscher Architekten (1983) and of the Royal Institute of British Architects (1994); he is also a member of the Italian Academia Tiberina (1978) and an Honorary Academician of the Royal Academy of Arts, England (1994). Throughout his career, Mr Isozaki has been active in education, and has served as a visiting professor at the University of California at Los Angeles, the University of Hawaii, the Rhode Island School of Design, Columbia University, Harvard University and Yale University.

## Fredric Jameson

American cultural theorist. At Duke University, he is the William A. Lane, Jr, Professor of Comparative Literature and the chair of the Duke Program in Literature. He received his BA from Haverford College in 1954 and his MA (1956) and PhD (1960) from Yale University. He has taught at Harvard University (1959–67), the University of California at San Diego (1967–76), Yale University (1976–83), and the University of California at Santa Cruz (1983–85). Professor Jameson's teachings cover modernism, Third World literature and cinema, Marx and Freud, the modern French novel and cinema and the Frankfurt school. Among his ongoing concerns is the need to analyze literature as an encoding of political and social imperatives and the interpretation of modernist and postmodernist assumptions through a rethinking of Marxist methodology. His most recent books include *Late Marxism* (1990), *Signatures of the Visible* (1990), *Postmodernism, or The Cultural Logic of Late Capitalism* (1991), *The Geopolitical Aesthetic* (1992) and *Seeds of Time* (1994). He also chairs the editorial board of *South Atlantic Quarterly*.

## Romi Khosla

Indian architect who received a BA in economics from the University of Cambridge and qualified as an architect at the Architectural Association, London. Mr Khosla founded GRUP (Group for Rural and Urban Planning) in Delhi in 1974, and has designed a number of large institutional complexes as well as small, community-based rural projects. His recent work includes developmental and revitalization projects for the United Nations Development Programme (UNDP) in Central Asia, Tibet and Egypt, and for the Government of India in the Himalayan belt. Mr Khosla's published works include *Buddhist Monasteries in Western Himalayas* (1979). He served as professional adviser for the Aga Khan Trust for Culture's International Competition for Ideas on the Revitalization of Samarkand. Mr Khosla was a member of the Award Technical Review for the 1986, 1989 and 1992 cycles.

## Yuswadi Saliya

Indonesian architect and educator, graduated from the Bandung Institute of Technology (Institut Teknologi Bandung – ITB) in 1966, and was awarded a master's degree in architecture in 1975 from the University of Hawaii at Manoa, concentrating on the spatial organization of traditional Balinese architecture. Mr Saliya has been continuously associated as an instructor with ITB since his graduation. Currently, he is a senior lecturer in theory, criticism and history for both the undergraduate and graduate programmes in architecture and is the senior editor for critical analyses of important Indonesian architects prepared for the graduate programme and published by the Institute of Indonesian Architectural History (Lembaga Sejarah Arsitektur Indonesia – LSAI). Mr Saliya currently chairs the LSAI, which was established in Bandung in 1989 and now conducts yearly national workshops to improve the ways and means of teaching history in architectural schools. Mr Saliya is also a practising architect, and one of six founding partners in the design office PT Atelier Enam, established in Jakarta in 1969.

## Dogan Tekeli

Turkish architect, has been in private practice with his partner, Sami Sisa, since 1952, when they graduated from Istanbul Technical University. Mr Tekeli lectured in architectural design at the Maçka School of Architecture and Engineering of Istanbul Technical University, and was president of the Chamber of Turkish Architects for one term in 1957. Mr Tekeli and his partner have won more than twenty design competitions in Turkey, most of which have been realized. Among their works are the environmental design for the Fortress of Rumelia, a market complex in Istanbul (Manifaturacilar çarsisi), Lassa Tyre Factory in Izmit and the Halkbank Headquarters in Ankara; they are currently working on an international passenger terminal for Antalya Airport. Mr Tekeli was a consultant to the Municipality of Istanbul from 1985 to 1988, and is a member of the board of the Turkish Association of Consulting Engineers and Architects. The works of Sami Sisa and Dogan Tekeli are published in two monographs, *Architectural Works* (1974) and *Projects and Buildings* (1995). In 1995 Messrs Tekeli and Sisa were awarded the Fourth National Grand Prize of Architecture by the Turkish Chamber of Architects. Mr Tekeli served as a member of the 1992 Award Master Jury and the 1995 Award Steering Committee.

# The 1998 Award Technical Review

### Hana Alamuddin
Lebanese architect trained at Thames Polytechnic (1983–85) and at the Aga Khan Program for Islamic Architecture at Harvard University and the Massachusetts Institute of Technology (1985–87), where she received an MSc in architecture studies. Ms Alamuddin has worked in a private practice in Lebanon since 1993. She is an instructor at the American University of Beirut where she teaches an urban design studio.

### Mohammad Al-Asad
Jordanian architect and architectural historian and is currently a faculty member of the department of architecture at the University of Jordan. Dr Al-Asad has taught at Harvard University, the Massachusetts Institute of Technology and Princeton University, and practised architecture in Jordan.

### Khaled Asfour
Egyptian architect and associate professor of architecture at King Faisal University's College of Architecture and Planning in Dammam, Saudi Arabia. He received a PhD in architecture from the Massachusetts Institute of Technology (MIT) in 1991, and an MSc in architecture studies from the Aga Khan Program for Islamic Architecture at Harvard University and MIT in 1987; Dr Asfour's undergraduate training in architecture was at Cairo University.

### Lailun Nahar Ekram
Bangladeshi architect who graduated from the Bangladesh University of Engineering and Technology (BUET) and continued her studies at the State University of New York at Buffalo, where she received a master's degree in 1982. She is the principal architect and managing director of Engineers and Consultants Bangladesh Limited. Ms Ekram has also served as a consultant for planning, water supply and housing for the Planning Commission of Bangladesh.

### Homeyra Ettehadieh
Iranian architect and the managing director and chief architect of the firm Y. Ettehadieh & Partners, Consulting Architects and Engineers. Ms Ettehadieh was trained at the Ecole des Beaux-Arts in Paris (1973–80) and worked in architectural offices in Paris and Montreal prior to returning to Tehran in 1989.

### Omar A. Hallaj
Syrian architect in private practice in Aleppo, with a particular interest in housing. Mr Hallaj is also a consultant for the rehabilitation of the Old City of Aleppo, where he is preparing detailed local plans and supervising implementation procedures for developing historic neighbourhoods.

### Mukhtar Husain
Pakistani architect and urban designer in private practice in Karachi. Previously he was the executive director of the Indus Valley School of Art and Architecture in Karachi, and chief architect of the Karachi firm NESPAK. Mr Husain was trained in architecture at the Middle East Technical University in Ankara, where he received bachelor's (1971) and master's (1972) degrees.

### Ralph Mills-Tettey
Ghanaian architect who taught at the University of Ife, Nigeria, as a professor of architecture and served as dean of the faculty of environmental design. He returned to Ghana in 1997 where he is a consulting architect specializing in housing and urban development, rural housing and construction technology and resettlement planning and housing. Professor Mills-Tettey is also the management coordinator of the Ghana Institute of Architects.

### Ildar N. Sabitov
Russian architect and instructor who graduated from the Moscow Architectural Institute in 1976, and is now head of the department of architecture at Ufa Oil University in Bashkortostan. Dr Sabitov is the chief architect of the Central Muslim Spiritual Board for Russia and the European members of the Commonweath of Independent States.

### Budi Sukada
Indonesian architect and instructor and the vice-president for foreign affairs of the Indonesian Institute of Architects and a co-founder of the Institute of Indonesian Architectural History. Mr Sukada also works in urban design and has served as a consultant to the Jakarta Municipal Government.

### Fernando Varanda
Portuguese architect who graduated in architecture from the Lisbon School of Fine Arts in 1968 and received a master's degree from New York University in 1971 and a PhD from Durham University, England, in 1995. He is currently a professor in the department of urbanism at the Universidade Lusófona in Lisbon. Dr Varanda is also in private practice in Lisbon with a variety of projects for the public and private sector.

### Aysil Yavuz
Turkish restoration architect who trained in architecture, with PhD specialization in conservation. Since its foundation, Dr Yavuz has been a staff member of the department of restoration at Middle East Technical University in Ankara, where she teaches restoration design and historic structural systems and serves as a thesis director for master's and doctoral candidates.

# The Aga Khan Award for Architecture

**Suha Özkan**

Secretary general of the Aga Khan Award for Architecture. A Turkish architect and historian of architectural theory, he was trained at the Middle East Technical University (METU) in Ankara and at the Architectural Association in London. At the METU, he taught architectural design and design theory for fifteen years, and became associate dean of the faculty of architecture in 1978; he was appointed vice-president of the university in 1979. With the Aga Khan Award for Architecture in Geneva, Dr Özkan served as deputy secretary general from 1983 to 1990, and has been secretary general since 1991.

Jack Kennedy, Executive Officer
Farrokh Derakhshani, Director of Award Procedures
Shiraz Allibhai, Documentation Architect
Marco Christov, Documentation Architect
Françoise Rybin, Executive Secretary
Christine Garnier, Award Procedures Secretary

# Photo Credits

Pages 26–29: courtesy of Saleh Al-Hathloul

Pages 34–35: Abdelhalim I Abdelhalim

Pages 38–53 Rehabilitation of Hebron Old Town: Güven Incirlioglu; courtesy of the Hebron Rehabilitation Committee

Pages 54–65 Slum Networking of Indore City: Ram Rahman; Yatin Pandya; Himanshu Parikh

Pages 66–81 Lepers Hospital: Ram Rahman; Per Christian Brynildsen & Jan Olav Jensen

Pages 82–95 Salinger Residence: Satoshi Asakawa; Jimmy Lim

Pages 96–113 Tuwaiq Palace: Mohammad Akram; Reha Günay; courtesy of Khaled Asfour

Pages 114–27 Alhamra Arts Council: Samir Saddi; Has-Saan Gardezi

Pages 128–43 Vidhan Bhavan: Ram Rahman; Rahul Mehrotra; Rominton Irani

Pages 158–67: Jacques Bétant; Christopher Little; Reha Günay; K L Ng; Kamran Adle; Mohammad Akram

Drawings provided by architects and redrawn by Darab Diba with Houshang Amir Ardalan and Amanollah Afkham Ebrahimi